Warrior

OTHER BOOKS BY THE AUTHORS

FOSTER
WILDERNESS TAILS

GARRISON
A PASSION FOR POETRY
PASSION LAUGHS OUT LOUD!
THE RUBY CAT

FOR SAWYER

How enormous to be like him,
filled with such confidence that he almost seems cocky;
not just overcoming fear, but rising so far above it,
it is never even noticed;
pressing forward with so much energy
that procrastination becomes obsolete;
using obstacles as stepping stones,
while running knee-deep in success;
smiling at both friends and foes with eyes sparkling,
clear of deception and challenge,
forging both loyalty and surrender upon contact;
and needing no inspiration,
being the inspiration for all who see him.

(Excerpt taken from
Farewell Autumn by M.O. Garrison
©A Passion For Poetry, 2013)

Warrior

The Sawyer Grooms Story, Wildland Fire fighter,
Fallen In the Line of Duty
February 14, 1990 – May 2, 2016

*"He could light a fire in you to love him, be angry with him
or be inspired by him. He was a fire in us all."* –Bruce Purcell

"Nemo vi vest qui mundum non."
"A man is not a man who does not make the world better."

By

Marilyn Garrison & Myra Foster

With Contributions from the Love of His Life

Lilly Rose Duffy

authorHOUSE®

AuthorHouse™
1663 Liberty Drive
Bloomington, IN 47403
www.authorhouse.com
Phone: 1 (800) 839-8640

Published by AuthorHouse 11/12/2018

ISBN: 978-1-5462-5726-4 (sc)
ISBN: 978-1-5462-5725-7 (e)

Library of Congress Control Number: 2018910123

Print information available on the last page.

DEDICATION

To the fallen, and to those left behind.

*"I still pray for all those guys on the fire crew
he loved so much." –Coral Rowley*

Also, to Sawyer's grandmother and grandfather...
who gave and gave and gave their love, their wisdom, their home,
their humor, their touch, their reassurance. Without them,
he would not have become the man you knew;

To laughter...
Sawyer knew the absolute necessity of laughter and its healing power.
"He could always make you laugh (and if you listen for it,
you might hear him laugh on every page);"

To Sawyer's great God—all-wise, all-powerful, unfailing, unstoppable—
The Promise Keeper, The Protector, The Forgiver,
The Eternal and Loving Father;
to the living, unchangeable, life-changing Bible that changed Sawyer;
and to Jesus Christ who never gave up on Sawyer,
and who never gives up on us.

SPECIAL THANKS
A special thanks to all those who contributed to these pages:
To Sawyer's family, to his friends, to those he worked with and loved,
to the love of his life, Lilly, and to all who shared
their life connections with him;
and to Adam Garrison for all his technical advice and assistance,
without which the book would not have been published.

NOTE:
All the post ellipsis sub-headings in quotes throughout the book
are taken from Sawyer's own musings.

NOTE
Scripture is taken from the New International Version Bible.
Contact the author at iron.pen.industries.books@gmail.com

CONTENTS

INTRODUCTORY NOTES

PART 1 – SAWYER GROOMS
This book is about Sawyer Grooms, fallen firefighter, son, grandson, brother, friend, musician, encourager, amazing and awesome man.

"With a heavy heart and sick stomach I am letting you know we lost an Awesome Firefighter; on the morning of May 2, Sawyer Grooms passed away at the age of 26. Sawyer became a firefighter at the age of 19 and worked with us here at Great Lakes Agency since. Many of you have worked with him and know what a beautiful, kind, humorous, talented man he was. He always had a swagger about him that screamed Awesomeness! This spring, five others and myself had been traveling and doing RX burns with him at Shakopee, Ho-Chunk, Prairie Island, Upper Sioux, Lower Sioux, Sac and Fox, Menominee, Lac Courte Oreilles tribes. I have set up a shared photo album for people to post and view photos. https://goo.gl/photos/rDkLGcjGcKECEMrC6.
PEACE AND KINDNESS TO ALL."
–Dave Pergolski, Fire and Fuels Manager,
BIA, Great Lakes Agency.

PART 2 – SAWYER GROOMS AND GOD
This book is how God worked in and through Sawyer Grooms, and the people he touched. It walks the steps of a proud, self-reliant man being transformed into a humble servant who learned total reliance upon God.

Not everyone who knew Sawyer or who reads this book has the same religious beliefs as Sawyer did. But since his beliefs were important to him, this book will share them as much as they pertain to Sawyer. This book was written to honor Sawyer, his accomplishments, what made him who he was, and what and who he loved.

At age six, Sawyer became a warrior for God—'born again,' 'saved,' 'believed'—hence the title of this book.

"Believe in the Lord Jesus and you will be saved—
you and your household." –Acts 16:31

The focus of this book is on Sawyer's last four years – a time when God became a confronting force in his life, making him more aware of the difference between just saying you believe something and living it.

He came to totally understand how life absent from complete trust in God was no life at all and how great life with God was when the barriers erected by pain, selfish choices and personal demons were torn down. This was not just a new chapter in Sawyer's life, it was a brand new horizon. It was as if God were saying, "Behold! Your God..." "Look at Me, Sawyer! See me."

In spite of this, Sawyer still struggled with day-to-day faith for living, the kind of faith that trusts God to do things for us that He says He will. Instead, like many of us, he set out to re-invent the wheel by trying to figure out how he could escape his demons if he just tried hard enough. Certain sins had become routine for him, and petty choices had become his roommates—he, like most of us, hardly thought of them as wrong-doing anymore. Many of his song lyrics reflect this state of his life, yet demonstrate how God's grace and life-changing power had begun convicting him of his lack of faith.

He mentioned times his faith wavered, but this new conviction of sin and a renewed desire to trust God completely, and to share Jesus Christ with others was made evident by his refocused objectives.

Sawyer had always loved scripture, but now his interest was accelerated to the point where it seemed he could never read enough, as his NIV study Bible, heavily worn and water damaged, testified.

From a child, Sawyer had always shared Christ with others, "Jesus loves you, trust Him." But now he seemed driven.

> *"Then I heard the voice of the Lord, saying, 'Whom shall I send, and who will go for us?' And I said, 'Here am I, send me." –Isaiah 6:8.*

With Sawyer, it was never about how much he could get, but how much he could give.

PART 3 – ALWAYS REMEMBER
THOSE WHO KNEW HIM BEST DESCRIBE HIM BEST

"Sawyer was a talented, kind, caring, friend that will be missed by everyone that had the privilege of knowing him." –J. Lindquist

"Sawyer was always brutally honest and full of love.

He brought me out of some pretty dark places just by being there." —C. Pratt

"He was a great storyteller—the kind that could get everybody laughing— and laughter brings people together." –EP (Boise application)

For Shaggy, success was following his dream regardless how of many told him it was a "waste of time;" talking to and visiting those that were considered "undesirable;" dressing his "unique" way, no matter what!" –E. Grooms

"He gave me something I often lose—hope." –D. Bonney

"The days of heroes are not gone." –M. Foster

"The world lost an amazing man today. His heart was so big, his laugh so outrageous, his talent so profound." –M. Elizabeth

"He spoke seven words to me, 'Don't ever stop, don't ever give up!' He was never lazy and didn't let opportunities lapse. That wasn't who he was." –D. Bonney

"One of the best parts of my life was this man and how he would visit often. Even in death he gives me adventures!!!! Me and a buddy had it out trying not to cry last night. He always was the heartbreak kid but he stitched our wounds." —C. Pratt

"Every day I got to spend with Sawyer Grooms was a lucky day." –D. Pergolski

"I remember that time we penguin-wrestled on Halloween and I split my eyebrow open. That scar on my forehead will forever be an honor." —M. Elizabeth

"You loved everyone around you and made them feel they were worth something." –B. Panek

"The world was a brighter place with you in it." –K. Tribbett

"I will miss you every day for the rest of my life. You were and will always be my brother." –D. Grooms

"In a world where you can be anything, you were yourself." —P. Christiansen

"May 2, 2016 left a hole in my heart, don't know what I'll do without him. Not sure if it will ever heal." —A. Hyde

Authors' note: It's our goal that you see Sawyer on every page of this book... hear his laughter... taste his music... feel his heartbeat... see his spirit. Most of you know he fought against 'demons,' but not all of you know he won.

"They told me to scowl for the camera—I said that was one of my best things... learned it as a kid."
Sawyer William Grooms - February 14, 1990 to May 2, 2016.
"He will bring me out into the light and I will see His righteousness." –Micah 7:9b (Photo by Derek Bonney, used by permission.)

FOREWORD BY Sawyer's mother, Myra Foster

When Sawyer was three, he said to me, "Mom, the reason you cry is because people can't see your good heart." He believed God was good and everything worked out for people who loved Him.

His tender and good heart was not readily visible to many. People saw a young man questioning everything, one who didn't understand the rules, and they quickly equated questions with rebellion. Still, he was the one who dared to stand up for the underdog and love those who were bullied and teased, always attempting to achieve fairness in an unfair world.

He believed life was hard because he was Sawyer. And scattered all through that hard life were stones to wound his bare feet. Sawyer ignored his own feet, but always took time to bandage another's, creating some story to make them laugh. And were it not for the stones, we just might miss the joy in the journey... often more joy than in the destination.

He found convenience uncomfortable and illogical... never a positive; and much of what he chose to do was inconvenient. He would say, "Calm waters do not make good sailors." He loved the rugged trail; loved the 45-pound pack plus chain saw and drip torch; loved sleeping outside under the stars or in a tent, where he would tell everyone stories and make them laugh.

He had seen good people become greedy and unkind because they habitually chose the convenient. Incidents like this seemed to motivate him even more to do things the hard way, the long way, the way that earned trust and loyalty; a way that distanced him from those who seemed good, but weren't genuine. The 'difficult' to Sawyer had value without seeming difficult; and the hard way—the right way—became the 'easier' way.

People knew Sawyer first by reputation; and by that, they understood he was not ordinary. He believed comfort would breed weakness, and always said when he grew up, he wanted to be a rock star, policeman or firefighter.

He experienced ADD, attention deficit disorder, which may cause those who have it to either not focus at all, often doing poorly in school; or to hyper-focus, thus allowing them to thrive and excel in high-risk occupations. Notably, people with these characteristics were often warriors in historic cultures—the salvation of families, communities and nations... a time when warrior-kings were common.

Eventually calmer, more stable times ensued, and farmers—not warriors—were the norm. Schools not only catered to the farmer, but tried to mold warriors into farmers. Right or wrong, experts then labeled this glorious trait a disorder (ADD), presenting as it always has, its unique struggles and its remarkable opportunities.

FUNERAL ADDRESS by Sawyer's adopted dad, Ernie Grooms

I've been really paying attention to and reading ALL of the posts on FB the last couple of days, reviewing his old posts (especially those on tour), and the reality that was Sawyer hit me square in the face. He was doing what his heart led him to do, a simple act where many of us fail.

He had come across SO many people in his travels, and shared an adventure! He didn't care who they were, where they were, what they did. The stories alone are testament to that!

Sleeping in the car in some park, with only a couple smokes left and no more baloney.....getting busted speeding to their next gig...sleeping under the stars with a camp fire in some of the most beautiful settings! No shower, no electricity, no bathroom, no bed......but he was fine with that, and looking forward to his next destination in some backwater bar on the bad side of town.

For him, it was all about who he'd meet next and what would he take away from it.....bad or good.

To share his talent and his being, which is quite evident made an impact on many....instant brotherhood.

He loved his fire!! I recall many telling him it was a dangerous job and he might want to rethink his choices. Nah, not Shaggy! For him, being outdoors, hiking, working hard, and the camaraderie.... That was what it was all about for him, and he took to it like a duck to water.

We would sit in the garage having a smoke and I would listen to the stories. Another adventure added to his list of memories. He loved his job, everything and everyone about it.

Sometimes he'd let a story slip out regarding some of the things he and his brothers Daniel and David did as they were growing up. I would find myself smiling, not so much at the fact of what they were doing, but that they lived and we didn't end up at the ER.....much anyway.

I mean, strapping on an old army helmet, sticking a pillow down their shirt, and having jousting matches on pedal bikes???

He was such a goof!! I remember a time when he called stating that his car kept overheating and he and Lilly were stuck on the side of the road by the cemetery. Pauline and I get round the corner on our way to help, and what do we see?? His little beat up Subaru with a FULL SIZE pool table strapped to the top!! Whaaaat?? Pauline asks him, "Does your mother know about this"? That big cheesy grin shined bright as he simply said...."no, it's a surprise!!"

The following definitions of success are collectively the "norm" in our

Society today. Many of us have our own definitions, whether it be making the basketball/baseball team; graduating High School/College; having a house/car, or business; getting married; having children; or an awesome job that pays well. I fall into this same category.

SUCCESS
Simple Definition of *success* Source: Merriam-Webster's Learner's Dictionary
• : the fact of getting or achieving wealth, respect, or fame
• : the correct or desired result of an attempt
• : someone or something that is successful : a person or thing that succeeds

From Wikipedia, the free encyclopedia
Not to be confused with succession.
Success may refer to:
• Attainment of higher social status
• Achievement of a goal, for example academic success
• The opposite of failure

Now..... I'm seeing just how wrong I was. You see, Sawyer had an entirely different view on "SUCCESS". He found the dictionary term as flawed, incorrect, inefficient, less than, and pursued HIS version of what success really was.

For Shaggy, success was following his dream regardless how of many told him it was a "waste of time;" talking to and visiting with those that were considered "undesirable;" dressing in his "unique" way, no matter what!

If one were to tell Sawyer "stay away from that person, they're bad news", he would beeline for that person. Why? Because he saw something the rest of us failed to. He could see "worth" where others saw refuse, treasure where we saw trash.

If one were to say "you need to clean yourself up", he'd hit the nearest thrift store and find another outfit that went the opposite direction. Why? Because he wanted to, not to be disrespectful, but rather to show that his view is different than yours, and you are NOT right, although many of us failed to pick up on that.

I've even told him myself regarding his touring areas, that these are some bad places to be, and to watch your back, be careful, don't trust anyone. Well, I imagine many of you can see how that went!

I could go on and on with stories of our boy, as I'm sure many of us could. Good or bad, that was Sawyer. I/we, will all miss him. I know for a fact he loved the Lord, and has been fighting the 'good fight' within himself for several years. Some of you may know this, others may not; but Sawyer does have a relationship with God. It showed in his tats, his music, his demeanor, and his heart. I WILL see him again. I thank you all for being a part of his life. God bless!

"He was a lot—
miss him a lot." –H. McLeod

PART 1
SAWYER GROOMS

"*Sawyer was a beautiful, beautiful man,
but never wielded that beauty in an arrogant way.
Got mud on it, strapped big black boots on it,
put frumpy clothes on it.*" —HM

Chapter 1

THE MAN

SAWYER WILLIAM GROOMS

Born Sawyer William Dec on February 14, 1990, he was a quiet, sensitive, extremely impressionable child with an enormous gift for observation.

WARRIOR BLOOD... "PART OF US"

It takes a man to make a man, the saying goes... and though Sawyer inherited some of his good looks and amazing baritone voice from Myra's father, Frank; he gained much more than that. He learned to always do the right thing from this gentle, mild mannered Abe Lincoln-kind of man of action and few words; and learned to see and empathize with the pain of another who also endured physical abuse.

He also inherited much of his resolute strong will, and his unmovable, undauntable spirit from his Viking grandmother—a part of his warrior blood. His Viking heritage became a fascination for him.

And never discount a loving mother, who 'gives her sons more reasons to live honorably than a wise man could ever count.' And oh, how he would apologize to her for indiscretions and failures. One thing he did not, would not, apologize for was when he was right and the system's phony righteousness was what had failed.

CHILDHOOD... "ALONE"

Though Sawyer's childhood proved difficult at times—a misery which would cloud and darken many of his formative years, as reflected in certain songs he wrote—at sixteen, he came to a point where he could finally say, "I will no longer allow these memories to hurt me." In a sense, he was free at last from the subjugations, but not from the mental anguish and tormenting memories that continually tormented and haunted him.

Sawyer's parents went through a lengthy divorce, and for a time Sawyer went to live with a friend's family, which became his second family. He loved and craved the normalcy he saw there. He, of course, loved his friend-brothers, Daniel and David, who had first become his friends in grade school; and he loved Mrs. Marine and the Marine—the caring, constant father figure he needed especially at this time.

SCHOOL... "MY EARLIEST MEMORIES"

Sawyer was home-schooled until he was six, and was then enrolled in the local Catholic school. This is where he first saw Lilly and fell in love—he was much too shy to speak to her, though, for another 14 years.

When he started attending public school six years later, he met Daniel who was shoulder high to him at the time. The two became fast friends. One day, an older boy struck Daniel and made his face bleed. Without hesitation, Sawyer took him to the restroom and cleaned up his face. Overcome with gratitude, Daniel looked up at his friend and said, "I love you, Sawyer." This was the beginning of a long and strong life-time friendship.

High school was not a new story, but another chapter. Sawyer, defender of the down-trodden, put himself in harm's way many times for others. It finally resulted in his being expelled from high school without completing his senior year, but not before the student body elected him Homecoming king in his junior year.

Sawyer did attend community college the following year and earned his HSED.

FOUNDATIONS IN READING & MUSIC... "GOOD PEOPLE"

Sawyer thought of his two brothers, who had joined the family before he turned eight, as annoyances when they were young; but later took pride in their brotherhood. The three would mug for the camera for no reason, or when they played the witch's castle in the woods, or when they were making music together.

Grandmother encouraged a love of reading in all three of the boys by reading aloud the Burgess animal stories, which were part fantasy, part character building and totally entertaining.

Sawyer's favorite books were the Bible, biographies of musicians, mysteries, anything about the Vietnam War, other wars, and history, as he sought to identify with the past, seeking inspiration from like-strung men.

She would sing old songs to the boys every night before bed like, 'There's a Pawn Shop on the Corner,' and 'You Are My Sunshine.' Grandfather would play long word games like 'When I Grow Up...' and sing songs like 'You Have the Cutest Little Baby Face.'

Grandfather, an intelligent man, used words sparingly, and never told a lie. Even before he graduated from high school, he was known as 'Honest Frank.' Later, that turned to 'Honest Abe' because his birthday fell the day before Lincoln's birthday.

Frank was not the disciplinarian for the boys, but stood alongside them to take whatever punishment Grandma decided.

Uncle Rob bought Sawyer's first guitar for him and taught him how to play. Both Rob and his wife, Ardi, have always been and remain a ready resource of encouragement and support for the boys.

BROTHERS
(L to R) Bridger (6'5"), Denzer (6'0"), Sawyer (6'3")
"When we were little, Sawyer thought we were just annoyances.
When we got older, he took pride in being brothers ."
(Denzer is now a psychology major; and Bridger now concentrates on
music and sports, planning to study pediatric nursing in the fall.)

"I'm so incredibly blessed to have these three sons with whom my mom
would share her celebration of life. I love everything about you guys."
--Myra Foster

*(You will notice some repeats in these
two accounts, but both
provide information and insight the other does not.
Sawyer did not consider himself an author, but he was
a writer who wrote prolifically when he was sober.)*

SAWYER WILLIAM GROOMS
(Born Sawyer William Dec on February 14, 1990)
(Died Sawyer William Grooms on May 2, 2016)
(The very words from Sawyer's brown
leather, rawhide-tied journal.)

INTRODUCTION
"To start off with, I think it only fair to tell you, though I consider myself a writer, I am by no stretch of the imagination an author. So, go forth and hear my story (assuming you read aloud to yourself), or slam the cover shut and forget we ever met!

"The following pages contain the stories of my life as best as I can remember them. If you happen to be one of the people who were included and remember things differently, feel free to re-write your version in the 'note section' in the back of this book. Chances are I will never see your revisions, so it most likely will be more of a personal victory than anything."

CHAPTER 1
THE VERY EARLY YEARS
"I was born in the small town of Harrison, Arkansas on February 14, 1990 to Samuel J. Dec and Myra L. Foster. My mother was a ranger for Buffalo National Park. My father also was a substitute teacher at that time. My earliest memories are being in class with him, where my infant mind found it a good plan to tie his shoe laces to his desk chair and other such pranks.

"We also attended what I am now aware were Civil

War re-enactments, and not actual battles, though I'm sure were you to have asked me at the time, my answer would have been very different. We would also canoe down the Buffalo River, and hike in the Ozark Mountains.

"I would occasionally assist my mother with programs she would put on for the park. She even made a miniature ranger uniform for me.

"We stayed in Arkansas until we moved to Minnesota where my mother was transferred to Grand Portage National Monument. We lived in Grand Marais on the shore of Lake Superior. I remember visiting Grand Portage a lot, and many camping trips and water fall climbing up the Gunflint Trail.

"We built trails and a make-shift gondola over a pond behind our house, complete with an arch bridge with a trap door. We dubbed our invention, 'Raccoon Village.'

"I met my first friend at the dump, where we would scavenge for cool stuff. We found a couple of big wheels and became instant friends racing around the dump and later, our driveways.

"My parents didn't believe in the public school system, yet, so I was home-schooled; which basically just meant Mr. Rodgers, Hooked On Phonics, and riding my big wheel.

"However, being a young and ignorant child, I wanted nothing more than to attend public school. So, one day after an argument about whether or not I could go (an argument I lost, by the way), I grabbed a shovel, went to the back yard and began digging. My plan was to dig myself a tunnel all the way to school, where I would sneak in and be with the other kids. Five or six scoops in, I was exhausted and defeated.

"I sat there crying to myself awhile, and then my parents came out to speak with me. They said they were going to continue to home-school me, however, they would put me in with a group of other home-schooled kids. To me this seemed a fair compromise. This is where I made another friend. His parents had built their own sauna, which he showed to me along with a pack of matches. Then the idea came to try and start a fire on the floor and enjoy

6

the sauna. I've since learned that is not how sauna's work, though it is an effective demolition tactic.

"Not too long after this, my first little brother was born in 1996. My parents, now very preoccupied with the newborn, left me no choice but to create my own adventures alone.

CHAPTER 2
THE EARLY YEARS

"We moved to Wisconsin in 1997 to a small town on the northern-most tip of the peninsula—Bayfield. My mother took a job with the Apostle Islands National Lakeshore, and my father would watch my brother and me, and take on the odd carpentry job.

"I was pretty quickly enrolled into Holy Family Catholic School. I met many people I would know, or at least remember for the rest of my life. I met good people like Ethan, my best friend and band-mate; and Lilly, my muse and the woman who holds my heart. Of course for every good person, there are two buttholes to take their place.

"At Holy Family, I experienced my first memorable crush, my first time being bullied, my first fight, and my first time ever being knocked out.

"My first crush was on the beautiful Lilly, although I never got the courage to speak to her until about fourteen years later.

"My first bullies were constantly teasing and knocking me and a few others around. My soon-to-be friend, unfortunately, got the brunt of the beatings. The day I stepped in to try and help, I got beat up; but I also made a friend.

"I remember this jerk stole my tennis ball in gym class, so I beat him with my racket. When I was sent to a time out, I felt so bad I started to cry. I think my victim actually felt sympathy for his weeping attacker; we also became friends. We ended up seeing 'Flubber' with Robin Williams five times in the theater together.

"As soon as I entered fifth grade, however, in the

Sawyer with his own NPS uniform.
He was at home out-of-doors from day one.

His favorite position—up to bat.

public school of Bayfield, many of my Catholic friends abandoned me. I did befriend many children from the reservation. However, it seemed for every one friend I made, two bullies found me. After several weeks of coming home cut and bruised, my mother told me that she didn't want me fighting; but if I was being attacked, I had her permission to defend myself.

"I was in special ED along with a few other kids, one of whom struggled with reading and writing, which happened to be one of my strong suites. I would teach him what I knew and help him along, though he was a grade ahead of me. I never thought much of it until one day I was on the playground and heard, "You have to get him! Get him, you pussy! You want to be part of us, don't you?"

"I turned to see the kid I'd been helping learn to read surrounded by his peers, being taunted into fighting me. Now this kid had a good foot on me, and easily one hundred pounds. His taunters all held rocks (the kind used for erosion control) and taunted him further.

"It was him or me, I knew this. I was outnumbered and outmuscled, this much I knew. So I weighed my options and remembered what my mother had told me. I waited for the large boy who towered over me like Goliath to make the first move.

"The boy charged me knowing I would be unable to win by strength alone. I took the only shot I had, I jabbed my hand into the boy's face, grabbing this Goliath by the lower lip, wrenching as hard as I knew how. He panicked and took a knee. I was in shock, I think, not actually be-lieving that could've worked! My body went into survival auto-pilot.

"Nobody move!" I shouted, twisting the young Goliath's lip harder still.

"The pack of boys was frozen. Goliath still at my fingers' mercy waved them off. They dropped their rocks.

"Now leave me alone!" I yelled.

"No one moved. I gave the lip I held a slight jerk; Goliath nodded profusely! "Okay?!!" I shouted again.

"The leader of the pack finally spoke up, "Okay, fine..."

"I let loose of the large boy, letting him fall clutching his mouth.

"I walked to the jungle gym victorious and proud. After recess I was called to the principal's office where I was greeted by my parents and experienced my first suspension... a confusing trend that would follow me to adulthood.

"Throughout that year there were many fights, suspensions and detentions regardless of whether I was provoked or protecting myself. I was ultimately expelled from the Bayfield Public School system.

"I attended St. Louis Catholic School in the neighboring town of Washburn. For the first time I had exhausted available establishments in not just one but two towns. I would later find out it was not going to be my last.

"With the exception of a few sandbox battles for dominance, St. Louis and I had a rather uneventful relationship, until midway through my 6th grade year when we were shipped down to the high school for Spanish and band class. Spanish was a joke to me—why didn't they teach Ojibway? And band class was demeaning. I chose to play the drums, but on my first try, the teacher decided I had no rhythm and gave me a saxophone instead. I threw it in the wastebasket.

"Then there was art. It was fun for the first few weeks as I drew in black and white, hoping the teacher wouldn't find out I was color blind. Then we were tested over the color wheel and I failed. They may have thrown the boy out of their narrow minded, round-peg art and music classes, but they could never throw the art and music out of the boy. I knew that someday I would rise again."

DECIDE... "A GOOD PLAN"

Like Sawyer, we all have a choice to decide who we're going to be. But, unlike many who prefer to coast through life, he took the initiative to spell out that choice,

One of Sawyer's favorite Psalms
PSALM 121
"I lift up my eyes to the hills,
where does my help come from?
My help comes from the Lord, the Maker of heaven and earth.
He will not let your foot slip—
He who watches over you will not slumber.
Indeed He who watches over Israel will neither slumber nor sleep.
The Lord will keep you from all harm;
(He will preserve your soul.)KJV
The Lord will watch over your going and coming
both now and forevermore."

fearing if he didn't, it would be done for him by default, circumstance, or by someone else's choosing. Even as a child, he had already narrowed his choices to rock star, pirate or a firefighter. Sawyer may have been ADD, but he was organized, focused, and observant. Not many make such a firm decision at such a young age.

He was unique yet flawed and would tell you that... echoing others who have said as much. So, again, the purpose of this book is not to excuse or expound on those flaws, but rather to zero in on the recent change in his life—what caused it and its results.

Sawyer sensed a change in the wind, as he began realizing that God was up to something... perhaps initiating the long-awaited emancipation from the demons that had dominated his life for what seemed like forever. His song lyrics reflect this quiet epiphany and demonstrate the working of God's grace, and life-changing power; and what began as a 'still, small voice,' would soon intensify like a quiet stream on its way to a waterfall. "Behold your God, Sawyer!"

God was also using him in subtle ways in spite of his flaws, just as He had used the religious, the blasphemer, the anti-God. Sawyer was the hurt child who feared abandonment; a man tormented by 'demons;' one who despised rules that seemed counterproductive; and yet a man with a good heart who genuinely loved God and his fellow man, and ultimately came through doing the right thing... proof that it's not as important that we raise perfect children, but absolutely important that we raise children whose hearts are perfect and brave.

TATTOOS... "NO CHOICE"

Tattoos were one way Sawyer kept special memories and favorite Bible verses close to him. He would also write much more on his bedroom walls.

Memories included those who had touched him in a

deep way. The young girl he had tried to help; a broken, stitched heart; KFC ('kills for Children'); NNARKHOS (without a leader, without a head); Nemo vi vest qui mundum non ('A man is not a man who does not make the world better.'). He would tat verses like...

"I have summoned you by name, you are mine.
When you pass through the waters, I will be with
you, and when you pass through the rivers,
they will not sweep over you.
"When you walk through the fire, you will not be
burned, the flames will not set you ablaze, for I am the
Lord your God, the Holy One of Israel, your Savior."
–Isaiah 43:1, 2

"Yea, though I walk through the valley of death,
I will fear no evil, for you are with me.
Your rod and your staff, they comfort me."
–Psalm 23:4

"O, Lord... my defense." –Psalm 35

THE MARINE'S PRAYER
After hearing the news about Sawyer's fatal accident, this big marine paced and wept and wept and paced in his garage. "Why, God? Why him, why not me?"

He said then it was as if God slapped him in the face and said, "Did you not pray to Me to use him in a mighty way?"

A MOTHER REMEMBERS

My favorite memories as a child growing up became an integral part of Sawyer's memories as well. I grew up in the north where my folks provided many memorable adventures. My brother and I never had to be coaxed to go play outside instead of watching TV; and were taught to love every season.

I remember on a variety of occasions, my mother

Sawyer was killed in a single car accident. He had fallen asleep while driving home after two long shifts on a fire. After leaving the fire line, he visited with friends around a campfire before heading home. He fell asleep at the wheel, and when his car came to a sharp curve, it left the road hitting a large pine tree. The car was overturned, windows broken...everything in the car was broken, including a guitar.
Yet, Sawyer's body was unscathed... not even a scratch.

coming up to my bedroom at midnight when the full moon was shining on a heavy snowfall, and her voice gently telling me that it was time to go.

We would put on our woolens and snowshoes and go out into the magical winter night woods. My parents taught me to love the winter, to listen when she spoke—and she did—teaching me that each day holds its own adventure.

My parents were big walkers. They walked all the time everywhere. They would travel out west and backpack into uncommon areas. Even the guides would comment on their adventurous spirits, saying they would never walk through the isolated places they did.

My mom still walks 4 miles a day at 91. My dad has slowed down a bit. But he still walks in his spirit, and watches mom through the big plate glass windows in the same house where I was entertained as a child. Maybe their love of the outdoors motivated me to eventually work for the National Park Services. It's been a good fit, I've never regretted it.

My parents were like second parents to my three sons, who also learned about winter's magic, had many adventures on the 'pirate ship' (actually a hay wagon my brother and I first christened the Jolly Roger), and 'fished' in the pond in the woods, which would forever bear the name, Sawyer's Pond.

My brother, Rob, and his wife Ardi, have literally invested their lives in the boys. Rob bought Sawyer his first guitar and taught him to play. All the boys are musical. Denzer is skilled on the trumpet, playing for community parades, university orchestra, etc.; and Bridger plays many instruments and uses his golden voice for church and school functions.

All the boys had an innate love for the out-of-doors. Denzer and Bridger both worked the local tourist ships during his summers; and Bridger is on the high school ski team. So much of this is inherent, but all of it was also cultivated by loving mentors. The boys have spent many

SAWYER'S POND
As a small child, Sawyer would stand here, raise
his arms and say, "Isn't God good?"
(Grandma, now 92 years young, wrote a poem about Sawyer titled,
"If you could only See Me Now!")

Lilly Duffy and Melissa Grooms (Lilly was one of many that tended the 4-day ceremonial fire for Sawyer 24/7. "There were no tears around the fire."

*Top: Lilly and Sawyer
at the ice caves.*

*Bottom: Ernie Grooms,
Sawyers 'adopted' dad.*

*"A part of me still expects
him to walk through that
door with that cheesy grin
and say, 'Hey pops.'"*

Sawyer's brother, Denzer, holds the firefighter flag by Sawyer's stone. (Also see the firefighter supplies left by Jeremy.)

"...It's in a nice place by a river."

On a brisk fall day with the same spirit of adventure and love of nature, Sawyer's brother, Bridger, heads to the Porcupine Mountain Wilderness Area for a few days of backpacking.

happy summers at the house in the woods in Michigan, laughing, joking and weaving fast and sure bonds and fierce family ties.

"Because of him, I have good people surrounding me with tons of support. He was the BEST!" –Sawyer's friend and brother, Daniel Grooms

Sawyer's second family –
Pauline and Ernie Grooms, with David, Daniel and Sawyer.

Pauline recounts the morning of May 2, 2016. "I woke up this morning planning to have a great day, but it started with a tremendous blow to our hearts with such wrenching pain.

"We were blessed to be Sawyer's extended mom and pop, and it is with great sadness we confirm that he has gone to heaven to be with Jesus.

"We will forever be grateful for his sweet smile, kindness, love of life, his tremendous talents in art, music, photography—he was so gifted at anything he touched.

"I cannot express how much he impacted our family. We love you to the moon, and will miss you so very much!!!! We will see you again!!!!!" -Pauline Grooms

"He was like a son or younger brother. He'll always be with me...mind, body, spirit." -Dave Pergolski

"I love you and miss you, my Beluga!" -Lilly Duffy, his light, his love.

Sung by Bridger Foster (brother)
October 26, 2016 concert, from the play 'Hamilton.'

There are moments words don't reach,
There is suffering too terrible to name;
You hold your child as tight as you can
And push away the unimaginable.
If I could spare his life,
If I could trade his life for mine,
He'd be standing here right now."

"Each time the snow falls, I see the sparkle in your brown eyes—full of mischief and magic. When I see you again, we will sit on a porch swing with Lilly and sing three-part harmony. Thankful you are my son forever."
-Myra Foster

Grandparents, Frank and Coralee, 90 years young,
with commemorative Eagle feather, illustrating Sawyer's journey:
The wrap is black, green, yellow and red , representing his black fire
boots, green nomex pants, yellow nomex shirt and red helmet.
The feather was presented to them by its maker, Ernie Grooms, who
with his wife, Pauline, made the 500-mile trip to present it in person.

Sawyer's grandfather, Frank, went home to glory July 5, 2017.
Death separated them a year ago,
But nothing now can ever separate them again.

Sawyer's sketch of his grandfather, Frank, noting that, as a soldier,
'he had won the war.' He also wrote (without punctuation):

"One day a young hero was called away
Unafraid and willingly he went to a faraway place
To protect us from a Dark enemy
Over mountains high and valleys low he flew over it all

Not an ocean or desert could stop him
Then after many months he won the battle and returned
To his family on a little farm
Since then not a day goes by but what he relives the horror

Yet he kept to himself nobody knew what pained him so
Until he gave a document of everything
To a young boy"

22

Sawyer and Grandpa.

Uncle Rob and Sawyer, loving guitars.

"*Sawyer had style like constellations have stars.*"
—*Eric Iverson.*

"*Listening to him play while the fire danced and the stars lit the sky on the lake—there's nothing I miss more. It's impossible for me to describe how much that moment meant to me.*" —*D. Bonney*
(*Photo by Derek Bonney*)

Chapter 2

THE MEASURE OF A MAN

A HERO IN EVERYDAY CLOTHES...
"I CHOSE TO PLAY THE DRUMS"

He was large inside and out, and even though most large, gifted personalities, are too often too proud to be humble, he was down-to-earth personal; loving and lovable; uncommon yet common; a true hero that never needed to rehearse his heroic deeds.

So, 'what makes a hero?' What is the mainspring that drives a person to give, and give when he himself has been deprived of so much? And why did God allow Sawyer, or any child, such a painful beginning—a why we may never know; but what Sawyer knew is that...

"God works all things (*good and bad*) **for the good of those who love Him." –Romans 8:28**

THE PAIN... "WHAT DOESN'T KILL YOU
MAKES YOU STRONGER"

How do we measure pain? Physical pain is often measured on a scale 1-10; but what of pain in your heart... in your soul? This little rhyme begins to describe some of it:

"The pain of parting, pain of losing
the one you love, who makes you whole...

Becomes the yardstick measuring
how wide the heart, how deep the soul." -©MG

But what about the measure of a painful childhood, or scars it left? A person's own tolerance for pain is a player, but more so is a person's ability to put pain in its place... something Sawyer tried to do every day.

Another rhyme, *The Mask of Truth*, takes the measure of this sort of pain to an infinite level. Here are selected lines:

THE MASK OF TRUTH
©by MG
The pain I've suffered, God has paid it,
No need for you to curse who made it.
Give all for Truth and set her free...
Release the cords of jealousy,
Of I deserve, revenge and fair;
And know this world is vapor, air.
So, don't weigh pain too heavily,
Or measure wealth by what you see;
Because it's hard to measure air,
Or weigh what isn't even there.

A GREAT MAN... *"COMFORT BREEDS WEAKNESS"*

Sawyer was an example of a Good Samaritan mentioned in Luke 10:33. He was generous, unprejudiced, a champion of the inconvenient, instant in action:

"Whoever wants to become great among you,
must be your servant." -Matthew 20.26.

Sawyer turned that verse inside out, upside down and reworked it with the common thread of an earthy man who lived with and loved anyone who crossed his path— friend, foe or stranger: He served because he couldn't do anything else—it's who he was.

Sawyer knew God had chosen him to do *something*; and

God has always chosen servants from diverse backgrounds, equipping each diversely for the job He's asked each one to do. If Sawyer seems different than most, it's only because his job was different than most. He reached those many of us will never have an oppor-tunity to reach.

"... (God) has given grace... to each one of us... to quip His people for works of service..." -Ephesians 4:7, 12.

So often when God wants to send his message of hope to the hopeless, the stumbling, the lost, he uses a common man—perhaps that's why there are so many of us—and these servants seldom consider how much they can get from the world, but how much they can give.

It's been said that you can give without loving, but you can't love without giving. So, how do you measure a man? By how much he gives? Or by how much he loves... his compassion... maybe how infectious his laughter! maybe all of these.

A SPECIAL MAN... "GRAB A SHOVEL!"

"He gave 110% in everything he did: fighting fires, singing, laughing, praying; and when he prayed, it was like the earth trembled."
"He was a special man—one-of-a-kind."

What made Sawyer so special? Maybe it wasn't just one thing. Maybe it was his love for people, love for adventure, his mystique, his laughter, or his mercurial wit.

He was never too busy to spend time with you, and if he knew you were hurting, he wouldn't just look you up, he'd hunt you down—show up on your doorstep at midnight maybe.

"He always saw the best in people. Where others saw trash, he saw treasure."

27

"Sometimes he would let the other guy win. When you'd ask 'why,' he'd just say something like, 'Bob needed to win today.' He always put others first."

"Even when there was no joy, he made life enjoyable."
"Every day I spent with Sawyer Grooms was a lucky day."
"He could put me in a good mood even if he wasn't."

Or maybe it was his righteousness.

"He was no angel, but he was righteous."

"He always did the right thing."

"He always knew the right thing to say."

"He had more integrity than any man I ever knew, or ever heard of."

"He loved more and judged less."

Or could it be because he DID give 110% in everything he did.

"He spoke seven words to me, 'Don't ever stop, don't ever give up!' He was never lazy and didn't let opportunities lapse. That wasn't who he was."

So, are you ready to embrace this warrior? I mean, seriously... tattoos, cigarettes, recovering alcoholic? Wow, that is a big step, isn't it?

So, if you can't embrace the warrior, are you ready to embrace his work? I mean seriously... sit next to a recovering drug addict / alcoholic in church? Wow, that is a lot to ask, isn't it. (You probably already are.)

So, if you can't embrace the warrior or his work, are you ready to embrace his God? Oh, you say you have done that. Know this, in heaven you will embrace the warrior and the work, you will know each one by name and you will spend eternity with them, and love them without hesitation, if, in fact, you have genuinely accepted Him who ate with the tax collectors, drug addicts, alcoholics, and even the vilest sinners He loved and came to save. He sought out—ran after—those who were in need, and found joy in their company.

Make sure of your own salvation.

"...Teacher, we saw a man driving out demons
in your name... and we told him to stop...
"Jesus said, do not stop him...
"For whoever is not against us is for us."
–Mark 9:38-40

Warrior
(Photo by Derek Bonney)

29

Sawyer – on the edge.

Chapter 3

THE MARGIN OF ERROR

LIVING ON THE EDGE... "ROCKS"

How close to disaster can you get, and not get burned; how close to a cliff without falling off; how close to temptation without falling prey? Certainly not a choice for the faint hearted, and perhaps not the wisest choice for anyone when you consider the temptation or 'lure of the edge.'

That lure is exciting, it requires great focus, great skill to remain unscathed—a real-life test of your mettle... of what you've got. Many who are tempted to take up this challenge only think of the great excitement, but never about the consequences should they fail.

To others, the 'lure of the edge' is a frightening thought, as well it should be. But to Sawyer it was exciting and fulfilling. Sawyer's friend, Ethan, said Sawyer always wanted to take things too far. It wasn't that he thought it was good or bad, it was just who Sawyer was.

Sawyer did have fears... he feared those demons in his head—the videos he could never turn off. He was just beginning to learn to deal with them by educating himself, by looking at them square in the face, naming them, and leaving them powerless by knowing what they can and cannot do. He hadn't yet come to understand the process completely... he just wanted to turn them off.

Even though in school he was in special education because of his ADD, reading and writing were two things in which he excelled. As long as he kept his mind filled with something else—anything else—these terrifying thoughts that plagued him were at least temporarily silenced.

In his last year, he had finally turned over his entire life to God, admitting nothing he had tried worked. He had come to the end of himself, trusted God completely, and finally found the way to escape the lure of the edge.

Ethan and Sawyer walking through tanglewood.

Every Monday at Sawyer's house, his mom hosted a Bible study / prayer meeting plus meal. Sawyer and Ethan named the group the 'Church Ladies.' The group included a cop, a ranger, a nurse and a shop owner.

Many times the boys would join the group—they only missed if they were out of town. They would play and sing for them, sit at the table and joke, enjoy their discussions, and awkwardly listen to the ladies pray for them, hug and encourage them.

For the last year of Sawyer's life, Lilly also joined the group. After Sawyer's death, the ladies attended Lilly's graduation from nursing school. They could never take the place of Sawyer, but they wouldn't let go. We link arms, we walk forward together... always together.

Head in the clouds.

"I can still hear his baritone voice singing full throttle." –CM
"He made and played songs like they were his last." —BP
"An honor to call you brother." —EH
(Photo by Derek Bonney)

Chapter 4

THE MUSIC, THE MISERY

CONCERTS... *"I CHOSE TO PLAY"*

Sometimes in the summer, Sawyer would set up his music on the front porch, where he and Ethan would start playing an impromptu concert. People from the neighborhood would begin gathering in the front yard and listen. Some brought chairs, some brought a beverage. The energy, electricity and inviting sounds were always captivating.

As a musician, Sawyer's sometime stage name (because he liked the sound of it) was Sawyer Cohee—an ancestral native name.

His haircut was also native—the Huron cut—styled after his Canadian cousins, the Wyandotte (Huron).

Sawyer and Ethan performed over 75 concerts in their five years together as a band; everywhere from Wisconsin to Texas to Los Angeles. Whether it was one or 1000 listeners, Sawyer didn't care—he loved the music. Ethan would tell you he loved the music, too, but was more audience motivated. Sawyer definitely embodied the soul, sound, rhythm, and energy of the music.

Sawyer wrote over 50 songs—words and music; and he and Ethan, as the '10 cent Cigars,' cut two CDs in 2013-2014 with over twenty of their titles. Go to tencentcigars.com or Sawyer Grooms to hear more of the group's magnetic sounds.

THE MISERY... *"CUT AND BRUISED"*

Sawyer's childhood was a mix of love and freedom, pain and confusion. When he verbalized his memories, he seemed to recall and recite the happier times. It was his music that made him pry into the deep, almost forbidden, crevices.

Music, art, poetry, God's Word—the seemingly less-formulated sciences—have a way of cutting between the soul and spirit. The first three allow you to verbalize and demonstrate, many times in the third person, the truth that the fourth teaches.

Even though there were memories that left scars, what hurt him even more was abandonment. He said, *"Then you aren't even worth being abused."*

Sawyer never wanted to be alone, and when he was he said, *"He couldn't turn off the video of those painful experiences."*

When waiting for Lilly or Ethan or someone to come, he would walk the floor before announcing a half hour before they were to arrive, *"They're not coming!"*

He relished being remembered. He might say something like, *"She remembered me twice today,"* whenever Lilly would call or text.

He wrote prolifically when he was sober, and loved to research his ancestry to find similarities between himself and long-gone relatives, especially his Viking lineage.

He had only just begun to put his life story to page before he ran out of time.

FACING THE PAST... *"BEST AS I CAN REMEMBER"*

"You Cut My Wings" is a song filled with scarred and disconnected childhood memories, and his helpless efforts to find the missing pieces. He remembered bits here and there, *'I forgot what I forgot,'* but could never remember everything that happened, and wasn't sure he wanted to.

One of the reasons he put so much emphasis on

today, was because he could often see no solid footing in tomorrow, and his recollections of yesterday—of what happened in his younger years—differed from time to time... so much so that reality was a constantly changing mosaic with either missing, masked or misshapen pieces.

YOU CUT MY WINGS

You cut my wings didn't you,
Even though you knew I couldn't fly;
Oh pushed me right off the edge
Even though you knew I would die.
Oh, I know you did...
Yeah, I know you did.

I forgot what I forgot,
But I know that it's coming back to haunt me.
When I went outside to try
To fix what it was,
You said you broke every rule.
I realized right then and there
That it never was real,
Everything is so surreal.

You cut my wings didn't you,
Even though you knew I couldn't fly;
You pushed me right off the edge
Even though you knew I would die.
Oh, I know you did,
Yeah, I know you did.

I'm just always here on my own...
If you want to find me,
I will be right down the road
Looking down between what they

Have deemed to be my own feet—
Never really sure how they got there,

All I know is that they are mine.
I'll be waiting here all alone.

I just never could comprehend
Why I got to do the things I do.
When I was a kid you prob'ly kicked
Just kicked me right upside the head!
I never really could tell.
Oh, it's sad, yes, it's too bad.
Oh, but what can you do?
You never could explain the rules.

You cut my wings didn't you,
Even though you knew I couldn't fly;
You pushed me right off the edge
Even though you knew I would die.
Oh, I knew you did,
Yeah, I know you did.

FACING TODAY... *"I AM NOW"*

"Crossroads" gives dimension to a fork in the road—a crossroad in his life. As a result of adjusting his thinking, his priorities and his relationship with God, he also began to adjust his relationships with the people closest to him.

CROSSROADS

Looks like we're at a crossroad,
Ain't got nothing for the toll;
Looks like a dead end street, darling,
Nowhere else for us to go.

Oh, been driving for years, babe,
Yes, but we ain't got no fuel!
Oh, I heard it's been said, darling,
Trouble is up ahead.

Well, looks like we're at a crossroad,
Ain't got nothin' for the toll;
Looks like a dead end street, darling,
Nowhere else for us to go...
All right.

Oh, that fog's rollin' in,
Yes, to the center of the road;
And oh, I can't see a thing, darling,
Except that we're getting mighty old.

Well looks like we're at a crossroad,
Ain't got nothin' for the toll;
Looks like a dead end street, my love,
With nowhere else for us to go.

Perhaps Sawyer's fatal flaw was that he could not stand to be alone. When he was alone, difficult memories overtook his mind.

"Demons" is his personal and graphic address on drinking. What seemed warm, soothing and angelic at first, raised its demonic head in the end: *'Angels turn to demons.'* This is nothing new... an old Irish proverb says, "When a man has a drink, drink has the man." Anyone who has had to fight the demon, alcohol, knows it is not easy; his graphic lyrics attest to the measure of difficulty he felt.

In his last four years, he turned more and more to the little New Testament that he always carried with him, Drinking palliated his torment, but now he had found the cure. He had been sober for one year before the Lord took him home.

"For Christ's sake, I delight in weakness... for when I am weak, then I am strong." —II Corinthians 12:10

DEMONS

Oh, I found the devil
Deep inside a bottle,

And oh Lord forgive me
For every damn swallow!
Angels turn to demons...
Angels turn to demons;
Hope they fly away...
I wish they'd fly away!

Came all this way,
But I feel just the same;
I did it on my own and
Still nothing has changed...
Except for you, only you,
It was always you.

People say these trials and tribulations
Are from the devil's hand,
But no, I think his hands are quite full;
I think these troubles must be heaven made
And I quite the fool.

Oh, I found the devil
Deep inside a bottle,
And Oh Lord forgive me
With every damn swallow!
Angels turn to demons...
Angels turn to demons;
Hope they'll fly away...
Wish they'd fly away.

Looking back I see only pain,
Regret takes its hold...
I wish I could fade,
I wish I would drown!
I wish I could hang and
I wish I could rot away...
Oh take me away.

Life without you is no life at all,
I couldn't see it then;
But Oh God I see it now!
But it's too late....

Oh, I found the devil
Deep inside a bottle,

And Oh Lord forgive me
With every damn swallow!
Angels turn to demons...
Angels turn to demons;
Wish they'd fly away...
I wish they'd take me away.

(Footnote: "My daughter led me to Sawyer; and his song,
Demons, saved my life." -Lisa Johnson.)

FACING TOMORROW... *"I WOULD LATER FIND OUT"*

Sawyer was a musician. He posted the following on his facebook page:

I AM A MUSICIAN
- We are the people who stay up half the night to finish that song we can't get out of our heads.
- We are typically misunderstood and always underpaid.
- We spend more time packing, driving, unpacking vans full of gear that we do on stage playing.
- But we bring entertainment, healing, love and passion to a world that desperately needs it. And I wouldn't change a thing.

I AM A MUSICIAN and I love it!

"Make Believe" is the thought of a prayer. Unsure of where he is headed, he admits that he's in pain and doesn't know how much more there will be.

He recognizes he has sinned against God; but also, that even though in his flesh he sins, in his spirit he serves

41

God: *'My soul is black, but my intentions are pure.'* Yet, with God there is hope even though man's view is that there is no hope: *'Say I've got a sickness for which there is no cure, I'm not so sure...'*

Whenever Sawyer would struggle with this war within himself, he would turn to these:

"I do not understand what I do; for what I want to do, I do not do; but what I hate, I do." -Romans 7:15-25; 8:1

"I urge you... to abstain from sinful desires, which war against your soul." -I Peter 2:11

Sawyer hadn't yet submitted 100% of his will to the will of God; but had come under deep conviction.

MAKE BELIEVE

Pain snakes behind my eyes,
I hold my face with broken hands
And I imagine all my troubles are gone.
I was wrong, this is just the beginning.

My soul is black but,
My intentions are pure;
No turning back
From all those terrible choices I've made.

Say I've got a sickness
For which there is no cure
I'm not so sure...
I'm not so sure.

You held a loaded gun, girl,
But it's pointed at you.
I can tell by that
Look in your eyes

You don't have a clue.
You can make believe
All you want to,
Won't change a thing.

My soul is black,
But my intentions are pure;
No turning back
From all those terrible choices I've made.
Say I've got a sickness
For which there is no cure,
I'm not so sure...
I'm not so sure.

He loved the comrades with whom he fought fire, or provided hurricane relief. He loved those with whom he made music, he loved his friends, his family, and Lilly's family. But most of all, he loved the one woman who stole his heart from age eight—the unstoppable Lilly—Lilly, the game warden's daughter.

She could out shoot him and give him a run for his money in countless ways; but she supported him, loved him and saw his brilliance and shining goodness.

WARDEN'S DAUGHTER

Met that girl when I was young,
Didn't have the courage to speak;
21 years later I'm bowing down to her feet.

I fell in love with that warden's daughter,
Now I'm on the run and my gun is loaded tight;
Running, I'm running,
Running right through the night!
Long as I fell for that warden's daughter.

She is the sweetest thing you've ever seen—
I got tattoos and I'm kind of mean;

But her daddy taught her everything he knew...
Only problem is she has an iron side, too.

I fell in love with that warden's daughter,
Now I'm on the run and this gun is loaded tight;
Running, I'm running,
Running right through the night!

All cuz I fell for that warden's daughter.

I fell in the love with that warden's daughter,
Now I'm on the run and my gun is loaded tight;
Running, I'm running,
Running right through the night...
All since I fell for that warden's daughter.

Best friends – Sawyer & Ethan

Sawyer and Ethan – Jamming in the basement
studio. Music, always, always music.

The following was found in folder notes:

UNTITLED

Man of faith! Man of God!
Man of errors!
Hold you up! Break you down!
Trapped by terrors!

See the flight, eagle flight,
Man that's winning;
See the night? See the fright?
Man that's sinning.

Holy God, staff and rod,
Only Savior;
Heal my heart, brand new start,
New behavior.

Who am I that you should die—
Pay the price for me?
Let me speak! Though I am weak,
I am strong and free.

Fix the broken words unspoken...
Make the music, laugh;
Love you only... I'm so lonely...
Today is all we have...
Today is all we have.

Sawyer would sing songs of praise to God—would sing *"Take It to the Lord in Prayer"* on the fire line; but was just beginning to understand that God also sings songs of joy over him. **(Zephaniah 3:17)**

Eph- 2:10 In the Greek Translation New Testament, it says that each of us is a poem written by God (poima... only used twice in scripture). It seems surprising, but it shouldn't be.

Not only has God written and sings songs for each

46

of us, His pride and joy—His creation; but, oh the comfort it gave Sawyer to know He also has written each of our names on the palms of His hands with indelible ink that lasts forever **(Isaiah 16:49).** No wonder we are compelled by the Holy Spirit to write and sing songs to Him out of praise, gratitude and worship.

Sawyer's mellifluous, musical lyrics had a cutting poetic, powerful life-and-death flavor to them. There were things he couldn't mention or didn't know how to verbalize, but he could compose lyrics about those things. As with so many of us, writing was a way to confront and understand the conundrums he harbored.

*People listened. It touched them... it
met them where they were.*

"I was blessed to have had the chance to make music with this guy—he made you play from the heart." –DP
(Photo by Derek Bonney)

His music cut to the chase, was graphic, brutally raw and honest—his past, his fears, his pain, his tortured soul, his hope, his God—and people listened. It touched them... it met them where they were.

He entertained all sorts of listeners, some of whom had never been in a church, and weren't looking for a sermon; but who, without knowing it, were looking at a sermon.

"You are the light of the world...
"Let your light shine."
—Matt 5:14, 16

A Tribute.

On fire--
This is what you signed up for... this is all you know.
This is what you do. So, you go.
The woman who first hired Sawyer, Joyce Zifco, recalls
he didn't know the difference between a Phillips
screwdriver and a flathead. She thought,
"Boy, have we got work to do!"
His fire boss, Dave Pergolski, recalls Sawyer's first fuel mix
for drip torch, "It was hot... could've blown us all up!
Boy, did we have work to do."
During the mourning session after his death, the flag was
flown at half-mast at the debriefing garage, where he
was honored for his work as a respected firefighter.

Chapter 5

THE MINDSET OF THE FIREFIGHTER

THEIR PART... *"FIRE"*

It's your day off... you pamper yourself with the thought of sleeping in. Then abruptly out of a sound and somewhat restful sleep, you're awakened by a phone call at 4 a.m. You drag yourself out of bed, answer it; then splash some water on your face, shower, brush your teeth, and like a robot you suit up, check your pack, grab your gear, say a prayer; and with a blank stare you put on your coat, and walk out to your truck.

There was a buzz going on yesterday about this fire—a big one. The early call this morning was not a surprise—you had hoped against hope it would wait one more day. But this is what you signed up for... this is all you know. This is what you do. So, you go.

Car after car pulls into the lot... unshaven (the men anyway), unbuttoned yellow shirts—all barely awake, all gripping travel mugs, coffee steaming—shuffle with dangling shoe laces toward the debriefing room (actually a garage). No one looks stoked for duty—they look (and feel) like zombies—disheveled zombies. But make no mistake, this is the crew that has your back, doesn't quit, that will get the job done.

No encouragement posters adorn the debriefing room (garage) walls. 'Honor, integrity, duty' were only posted on the hallways of their unconscious minds. Their thoughts now

Bravery is courage without boundaries.
Sawyer Grooms – 'on fire' with drip torch.
Not the white collar... not the blue collar...
but the yellow collar—only the brave.

were about gear, packs, survival, and fire—ordinary people doing extraordinary work. It's always all about the fire.

Checking your pack and gear is like checking your parachute—your life depends on it. Four canteens of water, 5 nutrition bars, and a first-aid kit nestled inside.

Your gear hangs all over your body: goggles, gloves, knife, cord, mask, radio, hat, bandana, muffs. And every yellow shirt knows how to and has used it all. Most all have shovels, some a torch and/or a chainsaw, and there will be dozers on remote sites.

Your first pair of boots may have been bargain boots, but none you've had since have been. You will put them through the roughest, unsparing test they've ever had. Your life can depend on the quality of your gear, so, the first and final word for boots is, 'buy good ones.'

Transportation to the fire camp may look like a plane, bus, trucks or several vehicles. There will be a mess tent and a well-stocked tent for gear where firefighters can refresh their packs as they rotate duty.

'On fire' smells like smoke—choking and acrid. You resist going for your canteen because you know you will never satisfy it. Even when you're off duty, you never get away from the smoke completely. It's in your skin, your pores, your hair, your boots. And you can never wash it completely out of your clothes.

The golden rule of fire is that you always make sure you're downwind of it, not just for the smell, but it's extremely and alarmingly dangerous not to be.

On fire smells like sweat, especially after the first day. Don't expect clean clothes or a shower for three weeks—those are luxuries. And food takes on unusual shapes and everything tastes like smoke: smoked coffee, smoked eggs, smoked toast, smoked pie.

Strangely enough, the smoke reassures you that you're in the right place, doing the right thing—something that's worthwhile.

You associate its scent with everything good and honorable about what you do.

Beaverhead Deer Lodge, NF
Sawyer Grooms—firefighter... fully equipped.

On fire feels hungry. It's a test of wills... are you better than your rumbling stomach? Can you do this? The answer is always, 'yes.'

Fires are loud and hot. Although hearing protection muffs are seldom worn except when using chain saws, they can not only protect from noise but also heat. Firefighters anticipate the never-ceasing winds that blow sparks onward over several miles, and change with venom, placing wildland firefighters in the worst possible situations. Their training and experience has taught them to constantly assess wind, preparing them for almost any circumstance.

When firefighters go on fire, the fire boss has made a plan and knows where every man is at all times maintaining their safety. Yes, his primary goal is fire suppression, but his first and foremost goal is that every man returns home safe. The firefighters' goal is to stay with the plan and follow it through.

Again, in wilderness areas, firefighters work to suppress the fire, without necessarily quenching it. Sawyer often worked on prescribed burns to reduce fuel in vulnerable areas.

Coming off fire can be anti-climactic—tired, dirty, hungry, dehydrated and suddenly bored. Life itself takes on a different luster when on fire; and when the fire is gone, the luster is gone. Any coin is gold when you're on fire; and every coin is tarnished when you're not.

Sawyer's ADD made him an especially gifted firefighter. His love for the outdoors made him an exceptionally gifted wildland firefighter. He took pleasure in the mountains and forests—just being there lit a 'fire' in his soul. And his soul lit a fire in everyone else. Once he caught the fever, he never wanted to be anything but a firefighter.

Those at home know their firefighters are always just one step away from death, and yet they still kiss them goodbye and pray like their lives depend on it, knowing this is their choice, something they have to do.

Wildland Firefighter Type 1, Sawyer,
Squad Boss, Terra Torch Operator

We remember the 19 fallen Granite Mountain Hotshots who perished on Yarnell Hill, Yarnell AZ in 2013. They were trapped by a wind shift and were left with no escape.

A mother of one of these hotshots wrote Sawyer's mom a note expressing her heartfelt and deepest sympathy.

None of us knows how God will use our sons and daughters, but we do know He will give grace to help and comfort us in our times of loss.

HISTORY... *"THERE WERE MANY"*

I researched and am grateful for several various publications that have recounted wildfire history, underscoring how extremely dangerous fighting wildland fires has always been, and credit them for much of this information. They recounted how hundreds of fire fighters have perished in the line of duty since 1900. Also, how in 1957, a group chartered by the Federal Forest Services studied the commonalities in the fatalities. The conclusion of this study was in a form of a list of recommendations on how to improve safety and reduce fatalities.

1) Reduce the use of flashy fuels capable of quick ignition and rapid spread;
2) Standardize training materials, including ten standard fire orders and fire behavior models to reduce:
   a) a.) misread in a fire's rapid-change phase, and the remedial action to be taken;
   b) b.) ignorance of fire behavior due to changing weather conditions;
   c) ignorance of the phenomenon of a fire creating weather conditions within its influence;
   d) and entrapment.

Since then, communications with the National Weather service has been strengthened; the fire shelter was created in 1967 and made mandatory in 1977 (it has saved over 250 lives); Nomex fire retardant shirts and pants use implemented, plus helmets, goggles and boots.

As a result of the 1994 Storm King Fire in Colorado where 14 perished due to entrapment, the approach to wildland fire fighting safety made fire suppression its number 1 priority, whereas before it was considered just one element.

The recommendations and new focus were added to the established training programs by introducing extensive hands-on training and field drills where fighters were asked to identify breaches in safety practices, make appropriate responses to unsafe conditions, identify risk management practices, recite fire behavior/entrapment avoidance models/ methods.

However, because fire suppression has worked so well since 1910, there has been a buildup of fuel in wildlands, which has contributed to more recent fires being larger and more prolonged.

Ordinarily, undergrowth build up is quietly burned off, but this practice was slowed by public resistance. Since the Yellowstone fire of 1988, however, which burned more than 1.5 million acres—mostly due to undergrowth buildup—the practice of RX burns has resumed.

In 2002, President Bush signed a ten-year comprehensive strategy to address forest health and fuel load issues, including a long-range pledge to better suppression tactics.

OUR PART... *"AN EFFECTIVE TACTIC"*

In 1970, 382 homes burned in one fire in Laguna, CA. In 1991, more than 2000 homes burned in Malibu because more and more homes are being built in or near wildlands, an area now referred to as 'urban interface.'

Everyone who lives in wildfire territory can do one thing that will lessen the risk of fires spreading and/ or engulfing homes. That is to daily clean combustible objects and/or debris from a 50 foot area surrounding their homes... an area referred to as defensible space.

This includes building materials used in construction and on the exterior of homes. Examples of preferred materials are metal studs, metal roofing, stucco or stone siding, and wood-like decking rather than commonly used combustible materials.

It also includes the cleaning away of pine needles or any combustible materials that accrue on the roof; avoid using mulch around the house...stones are fireproof and require less maintenance; do not stack firewood next to the house; and resist having ornamental shrubs or trees within this 50-foot area.

Check with your local fire post for other things you can do that will help reduce the risk faced by wildland firefighters, the cost of fighting these unbelievably destructive fires, and fire risk to you and your home.

THE FIREFIGHTER... *"WHEN I GROW UP"*

"When he was sober and on fire (on duty), he sat with the buddies he loved, but wouldn't drink— he just ate pie and coffee." -Myra Foster

"Best crew I've been out with ever by far and it was you Sawyer, it was you that made it rock." -from Boise app

"He was extremely skilled as a wildland firefighter and by all accounts very well-liked and respected by those he worked beside." -Kim Bouchard

"One of the best parts of my life was this man and how he would visit often. Even in death he gives me adventures!!!! Me and a buddy had it out trying not cry last night. He always was the heartbreak kid but he stitched our wounds." —Clarence Pratt

"Honor." –Guy Ishpeming Migizii Defoe

"Respect." –Tommy Richardson

"I still pray for all those guys on the fire crew he loved so much." –Coral Rowley

ONE DEAD IN BAYFIELD COUNTY CRASH
One person was killed after their car left the road, struck several trees and rolled Monday morning in the town of Bayfield. (May 2, 2016)

LAST CALL

Last call is a tradition among rangers, firefighters and police. This is broadcast over the radio on the day they fall. A video of Jeremy presenting Sawyer's last call was played at the funeral.

(All firefighting personnel this will be the Last Call.) "It is with heavy heart we broadcast the passing of Sawyer Grooms. Those of you who worked for and with Sawyer find it impossible not to respect him and value his tremendous sense of humor.

"His dedication to his family and wildland firefighting was well known by all and highly valued. He impacted and gained the respect of so many in his short time here with us on earth.

"We know Sawyer will watch over his entire family, friends and loved ones as he travels to his chosen place in heaven.

"Sawyer, you will be greatly missed by all. "Thanks for the memories, buddy. I will cherish them the rest of my days and I'll see you on the Big One."

-Fire Captain Jeremy Erickson

Clear 1635-

Left: Tommy Richardson, Middle Jeremy Erickson, Right Sawyer. These 3 and 16 others marched in the memory of the 19 fallen Granite Mountain Hotshots.

"Thank you, Kristy Peck Lund, for carrying Sawyer's memory in the Tucson All Souls Procession July 4, 2016. Kristy was one of the first people to meet Sawyer on the day he was born."
—M. Foster

"It was an honor." —KPL

"He was like a son or younger brother. He'll always be with me, mind, body, spirit." -Dave Pergolski.

"When Sawyer left, he left me his firefighter brothers—makes the heart murmur tolerable." -Murt Greengrass.

"You reached out to me and told me how us firefighters stick together. The last thing you said to me was, 'Take care, lady, talk to you later." -Jenna Lindquist

"That beautiful hair! After fire assignments, Lilly would work for hours to get the pitch and twigs out of it." -Myra Foster

"I met him quite a few years ago when he ended up on my crew. I was skeptical about this young man with long hair they called Sawyer.

"As it turned out, he was a hard worker willing to learn all he could about fire.

"We discussed him becoming a crew boss—I knew he was ready.

"I will miss you dearly, my friend, and will see you again. R.I.P." -Lloyd Pete

"Thank you, Lloyd Pete! Sawyer loved fire and the crew and special people like you who took time to mentor him. Our family and Myra and boys will be forever grateful for those who took time to take care and watch over him while he was on fire duty. He was in great hands! Lots of love for all the firemen!!" -Pauline Grooms

"Tragically, we lost a great guy today. Have some great memories of wild fires and deep conversation— jam while you can." -Gordon Robertson

*Boise Hot Shots
putting in Sawyer's
marker.*

"We never say good-bye, just let me hold the light;
promise that I'll see you beyond the walls of time."
–Jeremy Erickson

"He was a fireball, destined to burn
brightly and quickly." –Bruce Purcell

Condolences from MENOMINEE NATION.

May 4 is St. Florian's Day,
The Patron Saint of Firefighters.
It is also International
Firefighter's Day

Sawyer (L) and fellow firefighter friends with drip torches,
Jerry Jones and Dave Pergolski.

The Wildland Firefighter's lounge chair.

"*Best crew I've been out with ever by far and it was you Sawyer, it was you that made it rock.*" –EP, Markerapplication

"*Awesome firefighter! Awesome friend!*" –Ron Waukau

From the Granite Mt. Hot Shots tee: "*It's not what stands in front of you, it's who stands beside you.*"

Crew before heading out. (Sawyer is in back row, 2nd from right.)

Top: firefighters walking to work.
Bottom: Firefighters at work.

"Brothers 4 life." –JE *(Jeremy visited Sawyer's resting place in Michigan and laid down firefighter supplies.)*

"Love you, brother." –DP *(Dave Pergolski and Eric Adams planted a prairie garden in honor of Sawyer.)*

Dave and Jessica Pergolski with beautiful Lake Superior sunset. "Miss you, brother."

"13.1 miles hauling my fire line gear thinking about my friends that have gone on—Sawyer Grooms and Jason Waqie. Miss you guys so much." –J. Erickson

The following nomination was submitted for Sawyer to have a stone placed at the Wildland Firefighter Monument in Boise, Idaho. (Placed May 2017.)

Wildland Firefighters Monument
Commemorative Marker Application

Person(s) to be commemorated: **Sawyer W. Grooms**

Date of death: **May 2, 2016**

Did this person die as a result of working on a wildland fire incident? **Yes** X__ No__

Drytown RX

What organization or agency did this person work for? **Bureau of Indian Affairs Great Lakes Agency**

Position(s) in the fire community:

Wildland Firefighter Type 1, Sawyer, Squad Boss, Terra Torch Operator

How did this person contribute most to the wildland firefighting community?

According to Kim Bouchard, BIA Great Lakes Agency Superintendent,

> *"Sawyer Grooms was a highly regarded wildland firefighter who served on many wildland and prescribed fires for our office. He was extremely skilled as a wildland firefighter and by all accounts very well-liked and respected by those he worked beside.*
>
> *The hard work he did helped further the mission of*
> *The Bureau of Indian Affairs of protecting and improving Indian Trust Lands. In addition, he helped to protect and improve tens of thousands of acres of forests and wildlands across our entire nation."*

The National Interagency Fire Center posted a video to Facebook on May 17, 2016 that was part of a Native Report Series. This episode is dedicated in memory of Sawyer Grooms and features him burning a tall grass prairie as he works with the interagency crew.

After meeting Sawyer on a western fire, a crewmember stated, "Best crew I've been out with ever by far and it was you Sawyer, it was you that made it rock." (EP)

The stone will contain the person's name, incident or position, and date of death. Please indicate any preference for where the marker is placed in the monument: (*Attach a diagram if necessary*)

Near water would be perfect since Sawyer worked out of the Great Lakes Office, a stone's throw from Lake Superior.

My name is Sawyer
and I'm a limited edition
Habitat teddy bear.

"*The Lord is my shepherd, I will
not want. He leads me beside still
waters and restores my soul.*"
– *portions of Psalm 23*

PART 2

SAWYER GROOMS AND GOD

*"Read the Bible every day,
it will give you strength."* --SWG

*NOTE: After working on / writing this book,
Sawyer's mom, Myra, and I discovered we were challenged
and changed by Sawyer's example, his transparency
with God and his genuineness. He knew and lived
the difference between faith and religion, and was
one of the most unprejudiced people ever.
He saw all men equally: all were unsaved at one point...
those who are now saved had gotten to that point already,
while the unsaved were still getting there.*

*While Sawyer sat on the porch laughing, talking to and
encouraging an addict who still believed he had a 'reason' to use,
and who still was loved by and beautiful in the sight of God,
we were in the church pew judging him, making us
no different than those we were judging.*

*In the following pages you will find Sawyer's favorite
passages from the 'Good Book' he loved so much...
verses that encouraged him past his own personal darkness.*

Chapter 6

THE MESSAGE, THE MESSENGER

Though not formally educated in biblical studies, Sawyer knew the God of the Bible, and knew how to share God's saving grace. And God's message to the world wasn't something Sawyer pulled out once in a while—it was his life. And his message was always straight-forward and simple:

"Trust Jesus, call on Him to save you.
He loves you and will never, ever leave you."

His encouragement was always based on the Bible:

"Read the Bible every day,
it will give you the strength you need
to conquer your demons, your loneliness
and your emptiness."

This is a note he wrote in the front of a Bible he gave to a friend:

"Dear Brother Joshua,
You once mentioned a seemingly unfillable
pit in your soul. I, too, have felt this pain, and
through countless trial and error, I found God.
I hope one day soon you will find Him.
Hope to see you on the other side."

His stumbling and flawed behavior, the coat of error

he wore, never stopped him from sharing liberally without fear. He had accepted Jesus as Savior, and even though God saw him as righteous, at times could still be hobbled when he focused on his own flaws. When Jesus shed His blood on the cross, paying the price for sin, it covers every one of our sins—present, past and future.

As he began a closer walk with God, it saddened him more and more that he had grieved God and the Holy Spirit by his actions—actions he often chose to dull the pain and silence the video playing in his head... a record of every wrong he had endured as a child.

"GOD LOVES ME!"

"God loves you, He can change your life."
Sawyer would say this often when he spoke with someone—any time day or night—he would simply share, and often it was met with, "How could He love me, you know that I've done terrible things."

And he, like Philip, would say, *"Come and See."*

Then Sawyer would remind them of who he was, and the things he'd done. And if God could love him, He could love anyone. He found hope and gave hope by being in the Word and trusting in God every day.

SPEAK THEIR LANGUAGE... *"INSTANT FRIENDS"*

There is an old story of a farmer with a big barn. On one terrible, stormy winter evening just at dusk, the farmer could see by the glow of the yard light against the snow, that there were birds caught in the fierce blizzard. He thought if he could open the barn door just a bit, the birds would fly in and take refuge from the storm.

He wasted no time putting on his winter coat and gloves, trudged through the deep snow to get the barn, opened the big sliding door a bit and tried to coax the birds inside, but they didn't understand his kindness.

Then he spread some seed on the barn floor, but still no birds sought shelter in the barn.

Then he thought, if I were only a bird, I could speak to them in their own language. If I were just one of them, I could lead them to safety.

And so it is when God wants to send His message of salvation to a particular group of people, or person, he often chooses a messenger who can speak their language. And even if the person didn't hear the message, he would see it. And after all, believing is seeing.

"We are...the aroma of Christ." -2 Corinthians 2:15, 16

TAKE THE MESSAGE... *"I TEACH WHAT I KNOW"*

And no messenger, except Jesus Christ, has been perfect—there's always something at which to point a finger.

Moses stuttered, and used that as an excuse;
Debra, leader before her time, was misunderstood;
David committed murder and adultery;
Saul/Paul was righteous, religious and Godless;
Jehu was an illegitimate son;
Abigail was a believer married to a godless man;
Jonah was a suffocating and proud prophet;
Josiah was a child;
Ruth was a childless widow;
Philip's daughters prophesied;

Jesus was a poor carpenter... He *was* the perfect Son of God that a lost world hung on a cross, not so much for blasphemy and crimes against the temple, but because His perfect life convicted them of their sin-filled lives.

God sent all these and more to take the message 'God loves you' to a sinful, hopeless, dying world.

THE MESSENGER... *"WITH THE EXCEPTION OF A FEW"*
HOW THOSE WHO KNEW HIM DESCRIBED HIM

If we were to extract just the adjectives used in this book, most from the MEMORIES—how others described Sawyer—we would find he was...

Amazing	Effective	Kind	Towering
Awesome	Energetic	Lovable	Tenderhearted
Big-hearted	Enormous	Lovely	Truthful
Brave	Excellent	Missed	Unforgettable
Big	Faithful	Musical	Uncommon
Booming	Fearless	Naughty	Unique
voiced	Focused	Neighborly	Understanding
Courageous	Funny	Nice	Voracious
Compassionat	Generous	Noble	Valiant
Confident	Genuine	One-of-a-kind	Vigilant
Crazy	Great	Patient	Willing
Determined	Handsome	Quick-witted	Wiley
Diligent	Harmless	Redeemed	Xcellent in
Different	Honest	Respected	spirit
Defiant	Honorable	Righteous	Youthful
Dreamer	Hospitable	Rugged	Zealous
Easy going	Humble	Scary Big	

HE RAISED THE BAR... *"A PERSONAL VICTORY"*

In everything he did, he raised the bar: firefighting, music, love for the out-of-doors, love for people, selflessness, laughter, work ethic, honesty, and his love for sharing Christ. It seems, though, that for each strength a person has, there is also a weakness. So Sawyer's strengths became weaknesses and his weaknesses became strengths. Examples...

He was physically strong, but wouldn't hurt anyone;

He gave away everything he had, yet what he had was priceless;

He emptied himself for others, but was the fullest man you could know.

76

And if we were to extract just the names used for him in this book—most from MEMORIES—as well as a partner, we would find others viewed him to be...

Artist	Free spirit	Neighbor	Story teller
Adventurer	Fire in us	Non-quitter	Soul winner
Brother	Good man	Orator	Teacher
Cat Lover	Guitarist	Opportunist	Up-streamer
Composer	Hero	Optimist	Visionary
Dare devil	Hard worker	Outdoorsman	Victor
Dreamer	Inventor	Prankster	Witness
Encourager	Inspiration	Pathfinder	Writer
Energizer	Just man	Presence	Warrior
Firefighter	Leader	Risk taker	Winner
Fighter	Musician	Son/grandson	Wanderer
Friend	Man of God	Singer	Zealot

UNFORGETTABLE... *"BRIDGE WITH A TRAPDOOR"*

An unforgettable man with an indefatigable spirit, indisputable confidence, dauntless smile, inexhaustible energy, invigorating excitement, an undefeatable thirst for adventure, refreshing honesty, genuine sincerity, relentless work ethic, fearless risk-taker, instant in action with a presence impossible to ignore and a resonant voice reserved for the gods.

It's one thing to praise and extoll a person's deeds and talents when he's gone, but entirely another when a person's persona, presence and praiseworthy acts are known and listed in this life. It's not a blind difference, but a blinding difference.

> *"From everyone who has been given much...*
> *much more will be asked."*
> *—Luke 12:48*

You can probably think of someone in your own list of friends who is selfless, generous and compassionate who would fit this description.

Sawyer was not the first to give much, but he did it with such flair, such humility, such honesty, such fullness, such vibrance, that once you met him, even briefly, you would never forget him.

LESSONS OF MOKANE MUD!... *"A CONFUSING TREND"*

He never excluded anyone, and was never afraid of the unlovely, the unloved, the desperate, the ungodly, or the dangerous. Although, the marine cautioned him repeatedly about situations that would be better avoided because there are those who will continue doing what they're doing and would try to convince him to do those same things.

He also warned him that because he had made wrong choices in the past, there would be times in the future he would be blamed for wrong he didn't do. That's just the way life is... it's as soggy and as unsettling as the mud on the Mokane!

One day the marine grabbed him and pulled his head down to his own, and held him there with great concern and heart-felt emotion for Sawyer's lack of discernment in these things. Without saying a word he wept—something Sawyer would never forget. Not many events in his life made such an impact on him before or since.

HE KNOWS WHY YOU'RE HERE... *"I WAS ENROLLED"*

God has placed each of us in this world in this time to be a witness in our own various circles of influence. As it was said of Esther, it can be said of each of us,

"Who knows but that you have come... for such a time as this?" -Esther 4:14

We cross paths every day with people who are desperate for answers—people that need to know He lives. People who are living in pain, who hurt, are hopeless and lonely need the hope, peace, joy and forgiveness He alone can give. God sends us, like He sent Sawyer, out to the valleys of need, to the fields of injustice with the voice of hope.

Jesus saw the multitude as sheep without a shepherd and had compassion on them, giving an example for us to do the same.

We are all messengers... *"Go, and make disciples,"* and we all say something even when our mouth is shut. We each choose—passively or actively—what message we're going to send.

A former teacher once said, 'When you talk to people, make them glad or sad, but always make them something.' Sawyer was good at that—he always knew how to inspire you and light a fire in you.

He had begun to share Christ like life was too short to waste one day, one second, one breath.

LOVE YOUR NEIGHBOR... *"I MADE A FRIEND"*

Everyone was Sawyer's neighbor. He made no exceptions—well, maybe the Pharisees of today (those who put on an act, pretending to be something they aren't). Whether you were his friend, foe or stranger, he loved— absolutely loved—people: the drug addict, the drunk, the atheist, the prisoner, the hopeless, the discouraged.

"WHEN YOU'RE HOPELESS, EVERYTHING SEDUCES YOU"

"When you're hopeless, everything seduces you," Sawyer would say from his own personal experience. He was always ready with an answer for anyone, or a word of encouragement.

He understood what they were feeling, because he had felt it, always sharing how he had found the answer to his own hopelessness by faith in Christ.

"PROTECTOR GOD"

Sawyer was drawn to Psalm 35, which speaks of our protector God. He sensed a need for a protector who was stronger than all his enemies and fears. He would pray for hours for God's protection.

He was drawn to the mountains with which his life was so filled; and had taken refuge in the 'cleft of the rock' physically and also spiritually—a cleft God provides for our souls til the storm passes. *(See video.)*

"He hides my soul in the cleft of the rock, and covers me there with His hand."-song, Cleft of the Rock.

HIS LAST NIGHT... *"ISN'T GOD GREAT?"*

Sawyer spent his last earthly night with friends gathered around a bonfire. Friends said he spoke particularly about humility and how important it was to God. <u>He mentioned two favorite passages specifically.</u>

HUMILITY BEFORE GOD

"O, Lord, our Lord, how majestic is your name in all the earth! You have set your glory (in and) above the heavens! "From the lips of children and infants, you have ordained praise (established a stronghold against your enemies... to silence the foe and the avenger).

"When I consider your heavens, the work of your fingers, the moon and stars you have set in place, "What is mankind, that you are mindful of them? Or care for them or visit them?" -Psalm 8:1-4

"If my people, who are called by my name, will humble themselves and pray, and seek my face and turn from their wicked ways, then will I hear from heaven and will forgive their sin, and will heal their land."
—II Chronicles 7:14

Sawyer had found that humility—the complete surrender of his own authority to God's authority; it had to come before he could truly see God for who He is.

He found Jesus was the answer to his greatest need; and he found when he give charge of his life to Jesus, he could be content even in difficult times... even when difficult thoughts came to his mind.

Make God ALL your life, not just a part of it; you might think you have no power to do this (and you don't) but...

"I can do all things through Him
(Christ) who gives me strength."
-Philippians 4:13

We see the amazing power and grace of God in creation and in our humble response. We were not created for the world, but it was created for us—we are the only part of creation created in the image of God.

Try to imagine what great power and wisdom it took to create the worlds... unbelievable. Yet, there is more grace, more transforming power in the saving of one soul— saving you... saving Sawyer—than it took to create the entire universe, and God wants to spend eternity with each one of us.

All I Have Is Christ
Portions of the song
By Jordon Kauflin ©2008 Sovereign Grace Praise
You looked upon my helpless state,
You bore the wrath to set me free;
And strength to follow your commands
Could never come from me.
O Father God, my ransomed life
Use anyway you choose;
And let my song forever be
My only gain is what I lose.

"Be strong in the Lord... put on the full armor of God..."
Ephesians 6:10,11

Chapter 7

THE METHODS, THE MEANS, THE MOTIVATION

THE METHODS... *"KEEP IT SIMPLE"*

He never tried to hide his past or his mistakes. He was honest to a fault... could almost bore Mom with his confessions. It was clear his conversion was not done in his own power; and not unlike Paul, who claimed to be the chief of sinners, God's power was the only thing that could affect such miraculous changes.

No one will ever know who or how many people Sawyer spoke to or touched, except for the ones who have come back and shared how God changed their lives because of Sawyer reaching out to them.

His simplistic approach to sharing his faith was filled up to bursting with awe for God and compassion for men. He did not confine himself to a boxed-up, memorized, academic, sanitized definition of witnessing; he didn't take a class, no one taught him (save the Holy Spirit)—it was as natural as breathing. He listened to people and seemed to make their heartbeat his heartbeat. For that reason, he always knew the right thing to say.

His method was to say it like it is, never gloss over the truth, get to point, never waste opportunities or time; yet he was never in a hurry when he spent time with someone.

It is a glorious occupation to share the message of Jesus Christ because God commands it, and because we cannot refrain, nor do we have to be perfect before we do.

Witnessing comes with a two-fold blessing, first that the listener will hear the good news and believe it; and second for the witness who will know, believe and understand God.

God also tells us who should share the message—'you'... all of us, and He commanded us not to be afraid. But for some reason, some of us find our knees shaking when we witness, a lot like Peter walking on the water, who, when he began to doubt, began to sink.

"How beautiful on the mountains are the feet of those who bring good news, who proclaim peace; who bring good tidings, who proclaim salvation; who say to Zion, 'Your God reigns!"—Isaiah 52:7

"You are my witnesses..." -Isaiah 43:10

"I heard the voice of the Lord, saying, 'Whom will I send, and who will go for us?' Then said I, 'Here am I, send me." —Isaiah 6:8

Sawyer would listen to you first, before he expected you to listen to him. So, if you knew Sawyer and he hadn't witnessed to you in some way, it's only because he wasn't done listening to you yet.

To sum up his method, it was trust in God; and it was, 'if it's important enough to do or say, then do or say it now.' He knew how to listen to people and he personalized each genuine, caring word.

THE MEANS... *"RE-WRITE YOUR OWN VERSION"*

Sawyer was always the first to tell you he wasn't perfect—'I'm flawed,' he'd say.

"Woe is me! For I am a man of unclean lips... (but) my eyes have seen the King, the Lord Almighty." -Is. 6:5

He shared his irresistible smile with everyone, and pointed folks to the Bible he carried, and would add, "God loves you."

This upstream guy was just the kind that noticed the needs of others, felt their pain, saw the emptiness of people. He ran after them in the same way Jesus ran after him. He took time for them, never once thinking they might not welcome him at 2 am.

Sometimes he would just sit with them, sometimes he gave them a Bible, sometimes he would pray, but he let them know that God loved them and would change their lives, just as He had been changed.

Belief in the saving power of Jesus Christ is not a get-rich scheme, it's a get joy, get peace, find hope, find answers scheme.

THE MOTIVATION... *"ON WINGS LIKE EAGLES"*

Sawyer was a great man with questions; with God he was great man with answers.

He found these answers in the Bible. He would say, "Reading the Bible will make you stronger."

He found himself drawn to Jeremiah and Romans. Maybe because he and the writers had so much in common— inconveniences and dire circumstances, were mistreated and misunderstood. He also said with Jeremiah,

"His words burned within me..."

He came to know God loved him very much... even when he didn't feel lovable:

"I have loved you with an everlasting love, I have drawn you with loving kindness." –Jeremiah 31:3

"God demonstrates His own love for us in this... Christ died for us while we were still sinners." –Rom 5:8

85

He learned he must have faith to understand God and the Bible; and that the words faith, believe, wait on and trust meant the same thing.

He found that God was someone he could trust absolutely with his whole life...to direct his steps, to protect him, and to give him power to overcome the demons that had controlled him.

"Contend, O Lord,
with those who contend with me;
fight against those who fight against me.

"My whole being will exclaim,
who is like you, O Lord?
You rescue the poor from those too strong for them.

"Let not those gloat over me
who are my enemies without cause;
neither let them wink the eye who hate me
without a reason." -Portions from Psalm 35

He learned faith is like falling backwards believing your best friend is there to catch you like he promised.

"Trust in the Lord with all your heart,
and lean not on your own understanding;
in all your ways acknowledge Him,
and He will make your paths straight."
-Proverbs 3:5, 6

"Without faith it is impossible to please Him;
for anyone that comes to God must believe that He is."
-Hebrews 11:6

He also found that God gives us faith, strengthens our faith, and nourishes our faith.

"Faith comes by hearing the message, (which) is
heard through the Word of Christ." -Romans 10:17

And he read that God had already done many great things for him because He is a loving Father. Matthew 7:7 says, *"For everyone who asks receives..."*

"Those who hope in the Lord will renew their strength.
They will soar on wings like eagles;
they will run and not grow weary,
they will walk and not be faint." –Is. 40:31

Sawyer read the Bible almost every day always yearning to learn more about God and His promises, and more about what God expected from him.

"He has shown you... what is good. And what does
the Lord require of you? To act justly, to love mercy
and to walk humbly with your God. "Micah 6:8

"Fear God and keep His commandments, for this
is the whole duty of man." –Ecclesiastes 12:13

"Love the Lord your God with all your
heart... soul... mind... strength... love your
neighbor as yourself." Mark 12:30, 31

"Do not conform (yourself)...to this world, but be trans-
formed by the renewing of your mind." –Rom. 12:1

And when his mind was renewed, his actions were, too. He not only lived Romans 12, he *was* Romans 12.

What a good exercise for each of us! Walk through Romans 12 and ask ourselves whether or not each one of these can truly be said of our life.

"Love must be sincere;

"Hate what is evil, cling to what is good;

"Be devoted to one another in brotherly love;

"Honor one another above yourselves;

"Be zealous (in business), and fervent in spirit...

"Be joyful in hope, patient in affliction,
faithful in prayer;

"Share with those in need,
and practice hospitality;

"Bless those who persecute you, and curse not;

"Rejoice with those who rejoice...
weep with those who mourn;

"Live in harmony with each other, and be not proud;

"Associate with everyone without being conceited;

"Do not repay evil for evil...
be careful to do what is right
in the sight of all men;

"If your enemy is hungry, feed him;
if he's thirsty, give him something to drink;

"Do not be overcome with evil,
but overcome evil with good."
–Romans 12:9-21

The greatness of God motivates.

"Ah, Sovereign Lord!
You have made the heavens and the earth
by your great power
and outstretched arm.
Nothing is too hard for you..."
–Jeremiah 32:17, 27

SAWYER WILLIAM GROOMS
"... smiling at both friends and foes
with eyes sparkling, clear of deception and challenge,
forging both loyalty and surrender upon contact;
and needing no inspiration, being the inspiration
for all who see him."

"I know the plans I have for you, declares the
Lord; plans to prosper you and not harm you...
"Pray to me...and I will listen.
"You will seek me and find me,
when you seek me with all your heart."
–Jeremiah 29:11-13

A year before his promotion to glory, Sawyer found himself in the fast lane with God. He was in church as often as his schedule allowed and spent hours in Bible study and prayer.

He exuded confidence, compassion, and candor—he was brutally honest about himself. He made no excuses. It did not suit him to live a lie—that's not who he was. But more than that, he had a broken and contrite heart, and like David, bared his soul before God.

He, though physically strong, recognized that he was spiritually feeble, and only in Christ was there power to live a godly, victorious life. He turned his greatest weakness into his greatest strength; he turned his greatest strength into his greatest weakness.

Unbelievably great things would happen if every idle believer came to the point Sawyer did in their lives where they realize that up until that point, all they've ever done for God was the least possible.

It's only at the moment a believer sees God... sees the greatness of God and the finiteness of himself, that he is changed forever. And it is then when God is ready to put the believer in the 'fast lane,' preparing him for a unique and memorable journey and perhaps a great task.

ALWAYS READY... *"A MAKE-SHIFT GONDOLA"*

Sawyer shared Christ anytime, all the time—day or night. There was no hour, distance, or inconvenience that kept him from appointed rounds; because it was not a separate mode he clicked into when saw a need, but an attitude that couldn't be stopped.

"Your attitude should be the same as that of Christ Jesus." —Philippians 2:5

"Always be prepared to give an answer to everyone who asks you the reason for the hope you have." -I Peter 3:15

Sawyer knew when he read the Bible, he found strength and wisdom to make right choices.

"For the word of God is living, and active, and sharper than any double-edged sword. It penetrates even to the dividing of soul and spirit... and it judges the thoughts and attitudes (intents) of the heart." -Hebrews 4:12

When Sawyer would tell someone about Jesus, so many times he heard, "I can't change. I've tried, but I still come back and use again. I'm not strong enough to do this."

It had a very familiar ring to it. "I know you're not, I'm not either. I ask Christ to give me strength and He does. When I read the Bible, I'm stronger. You need a Bible, too. You need to read it every day."

Then often he would give out a brand new Bible. He gave away numerous Bibles, no one here counting.

FAMILY... *"I WILL RISE AGAIN!"*

God made us... we are His creation. We are His joy. When we believe in Him, we are family, and it shouldn't surprise us that He is concerned about us all day, every day.

As a child, not only was Sawyer taught that always doing the right thing was always the right choice, but he was shown the love of God in people, music, guitars, writing, composing, and performing.

He loved laughing with his friends; and his music and humor were definitely out of the box—not like anything else... not like anyone else.

But what other people thought of, or said about him

never bothered him; and he would encourage others also to just be themselves, and always do the right thing. 'Be yourself because those that matter don't mind, and those that mind don't matter.'

In spite of abuse, abandonment, disappointment; in spite of his failures, faults and feeble attempts to fix things that were still unresolved; and in spite of the fractured, painful reasoning found in his music—hope you don't mind me saying, 'Hallelujah!' here, because—God raised Sawyer up above it all!

"I delight in weaknesses... insults...
hardships...persecutions... difficulties...
for when I am weak, then I am strong."
-II Corinthians 12:10

"I consider everything a loss compared
to the surpassing greatness of knowing
Christ Jesus my Lord; for whose sake I have lost
all things, and consider them but rubbish,
that I may gain Christ, and be found in Him.
—Philippians 3:8

"Not having a righteousness of my own,
that comes from the law; but that which is
through the faith in Christ—the righteousness
which comes from God and is by faith."
-Philippians 3:9

MOTIVATED BY THOSE AROUND US..."BEST FRIEND"

In just everyday living, he and his friend-brother, Ethan encouraged each other. They would camp out anywhere, and cook and eat anything. They would create spontaneous dialogue that made them howl with unrestrained laughter.

This was more like a pressure valve than motivation.

But no two better partners in 'crime'... but never bad crime. They were rough, tough men; but, according to the lovely Lilly, they were also 'two ridiculous, goofy boys.'

His motivation would not be complete without mentioning a few more people: of course his godly mother, his grandmother and grandfather and members of their families, aunt Ardi and uncle Rob, brothers Bridger and Denzer; his second family—the marine and his wife, and two more brothers, David and Daniel; his best friend, Ethan, a multitude of more peripheral friends and relatives; and last but not least, the love of his life—Lilly. She was his sunrise, his completer, his joy, his heart—and their loving nicknames for each other was 'Baluga.' He was terrified he would lose her. She was his love, his breath, his heartbeat, his life.

In her words, he was "sensitive, a sweetheart, always willing to help. He didn't play by the rules—even though she did; and he was so bad with money... spending all he had for the best music."

She remembered once for his birthday, he announced that his mom had made a great cake and Lilly had made a 'pretty good' pumpkin pie. His nuancical comments were so entertaining, there was no such thing as feeling slighted or overlooked. In them all, you knew you were loved.

So, there was genetic motivation—Viking blood, warrior blood; godly motivation—values and character, environmental motivation, and the unwavering Word of God. Even without words, all creation speaks of God and His greatness. And especially, there was the constant support and affirmation from a varied and textured cheering section.

All these worked together to form the man, means, motivation and methods. Some were learned, some copied, some were variations and/or composites of what he had seen or heard, and some were just down-right original. All simple, none verbose—not his style—he had no time for excess.

And lastly, surely the soul of the firefighter taught

him urgency, and that if you could shorten what you had to say in one word, then do it... like "FIRE!"—a message not often misunderstood.

JONAH AND THE WHALE... *"AND OTHER PRANKS"*

The ultimate motivation is God and His Command. Just like work...we value the comments or our co-workers, but we absolutely focus on what the 'boss' says.

So, like Jonah, called to go to Ninevah, when God had a job for Sawyer, he could find no peace until he did it.

Jonah was a godly man—a prophet who studied scripture day and night. Ninevah was not just a sin-filled city for which Jonah felt no compassion, it was a brutal and torturous culture. The ruins of Ninevah lie in ISIS territory of today, and these two cultures share many similarities.

Can you imagine the internal conflict he must've felt when God's word came to him to go to Ninevah and preach: 'Repent, turn from your wicked ways' so that God's judgment may be averted? Jonah not only believed Ninevah deserved God's judgment, and perhaps even prayed for it; but that it also was a suicide mission must've crossed his mind.

So great was that conflict, that instead of obeying God's voice, he boarded a ship going in the opposite direction! But when God speaks to us, He doesn't let go until we listen. He is compassionate, patient, tender, loving and... relentless. He WILL get our attention.

Jonah's sin—a lack of trust in God...believing his own way was better than God's way—resulted in the loss of someone else's ship and all the goods on it; and probably a three-day upset stomach for the fish who had to swallow him.

God did get Jonah's attention. Jonah knew he had disobeyed. He knew God so well from reading scripture over and over, and yet he missed one of God's greatest attributes—compassion. "Behold God, Jonah."

A refresher on how this story ends: Jonah does go and preach to Ninevah, God does protect him, the people do repent, and God's judgment is stayed. Jonah, on the other hand, still had issues with the fact that even though they deserved judgement, God decided to be merciful. Something he missed totally until 'the gourd.'

When the sun beat down on him, God sent an amazingly fast-growing gourd to provide needed shelter. Jonah was relieved, until God then destroyed the gourd, and Jonah was again miserable. God's lesson showed Jonah how his dismay over the loss of a simple plant could not compare to God's dismay over the loss of a great city filled with many people.

God is an unchanging God...He cannot change who He is. He is always compassionate, always merciful, never willing that any should perish in hell. And sometimes he will pair up the least likely messenger with a people who need to hear that He loves them and is willing to forgive ALL their sin, preparing them for their eternal journey where they will live with Him forever.

"Jesus Christ, the same yesterday,
today and forever" –Hebrews 13:8

MAN UP

Perhaps Sawyer's legacy has inspired you to find your faith, share your faith, bolster your faith, and / or renew your faith. As Sawyer would say, "Are you ready to believe Jesus for realsies?"

Is today the day that you will trust God completely, surrender to Him completely, believe Him completely. Are you ready to stand up, show up, speak up—carry on the torch that Sawyer carried?

"I saw Sawyer on Wednesday—he swooped in to say hello." –DB

STAND UP
"When I am weak, then I am strong." -II Cor. 12:10

SHOW UP
"He had to go through Samaria." -John 4:4

SPEAK UP
People are waiting to hear that Jesus loves them.

"Tell me please..." -Acts 8:34

"How then can they call on the One in whom they have not believed? And how can they believe on Him of whom they have not heard? And how can they hear without someone preaching to them?

"And how can they preach unless they are sent? As it is written, How beautiful are the feet of those who bring Good News (the Gospel of Peace)!" –Romans 10:14, 15

Maybe today, there is someone you can encourage; someone who needs to hear, "God loves you and cares about you;" someone who is hopeless, who needs to hear, "In the Word of God there is hope."

Be warrior...
Be a Sawyer.

"When does destiny first cast its shadow upon a child's mind?"
—Winston Churchill

Chapter 8

THE MIRACLES

Paul and Silas turned their world upside down for Christ, Acts 17:6, and Sawyer was doing the same for his world. He was not an overt, fire and brimstone preacher, but an encouraging, show-up-anytime friend with faith in his heart, a Bible in his hand, a sparkle in his eye and the good news that Jesus Christ loves you... and you... and you. Sawyer shared how Jesus Christ can strengthen you so you don't have to succumb to the bait of sin; how He can give you hope where you thought there was none; and how God will care for you when you thought no one would.

ROOMMATE

Sawyer put himself in situations and surrounded himself with those who could have had a negative influence—influences that would test his strength of character and his reliance on the power of God to keep him safe and uncompromised. He prayed and pleaded daily for God's protection.

Nathan, Sawyer's roommate, was one of those people. Sawyer pressed him often asking, "When are you going to believe in God for realsies?"

"Soon," he would say, putting Sawyer off for another day.

Because of his addiction he lost jobs and family.

There was a time he said that the only one who really cared enough to tell him the truth was Sawyer.

While Nathan struggled with addiction, I struggled

with judgement and disapproval. If Sawyer taught me anything it was that addiction is no different than my own repetitive actions that not only harm myself, but others. You see, I was no different than Nathan...not really.

"Sawyer was forgiving and loving to all, but I wasn't. I had seen too many people use and hurt him. Now...today, at the funeral, Nathan wanted to visit with me—I really didn't want him around me, but despite my angry heart, I agreed to see him.

He sat on my front porch and told me of his changed life, and how Sawyer had told him the only way to be free of his demons was to surrender to the God of the impossible.

Sawyer knew the all-powerful, all-forgiving God, but had not yet completely surrendered his life. So even though he was still struggling with his own demons at the time— he shared the simple message of salvation. If we waited until we were perfect to speak the truth, no one would ever hear it."

The following are Nathan's own words: "There was this moment. A choice. It was reactionary.

"The moments slowed down. My senses whirled in my taste buds. I could feel the end in every muscle. I had nothing left to lose. One way or another it was going to end.

"It was bright that morning. It seemed brighter than usual, perhaps because I hadn't been outside during daylight hours in days. The morning was warm. Looking back, the day was a perfect day to surrender.

"When the red and blue flashing lights lit up behind me I wasn't surprised. I don't remember exactly the thoughts in my head at that moment, but I was calm. I asked my passenger to buckle up and I punched it. I raced dangerously through the streets of Frog Town. One became many. Zig-zagging through the blocks trying to shake the black and whites behind me.

"I don't remember a lot of details in these moments. It was fast and desperate and I was surprised that they were staying on me the way they were. Looking back, I'm not even sure what I was running to. There was nothing left.

"It didn't last long. The roads were soft and had a lot of loose gravel on the surface. I came to a sudden and abrupt stop when the stolen car I was driving slammed into a huge oak on the boulevard. I recall watching the front tire continue down the street as if it hadn't missed the turn with the rest of the car. I remember wondering why the airbags hadn't erupted.

"There was a lot of noise and yelling. I was pulled by gunpoint from the vehicle. The officer must have been a rookie. He was trembling... his words jumbled and broken. I remember just going limp. "This was the first time I surrendered to my situation.

"I remember smelling the radiator coolant that was saturating the ground my face was close to. I felt empty and alone, though there were five big guys on top of me. They kept asking me questions. Rapid firing a barrage of demands. I didn't even have words left.

"I was pushed into a car, cuffed and bloody. The world around me went dark.

"My mind drifted into a dream. I'm not sure if I fell asleep or if I blacked out.

"I remember sensing my sons. I could hear their laughter. I could feel my heart break. I was sitting in tall grass on a hill. I could hear the laughter but I couldn't locate the source. There was wreckage around the base of the hill. I can't remember specifically what kind of wreckage, but now I realize it was my life.

"In a flash I was somewhere else. I was stuck. I was frantic. I was alone. There was no light. I felt like I was collapsing into myself. My lungs were tight. I didn't think I wanted to live up to this point, but now I was desperate to breath.

"When I came to, there was a paramedic over me and a detective. I was still in the police car. I had tears and blood streaming down my face. They were asking me if I was alright. I think I nodded. They were taking me to the hospital anyway.

"This morning was the end for me.

"The months following this I would lay in my cell at night and I could hear that laughter. It haunted me. I would replay all the horrible scenarios that brought me to this point.

"I knew I was far from human aid. I knew I only had to surrender to God the way I had surrendered to that nervous rookie officer. I didn't know what this looked like at first, but I'm finally getting it. Surrender is to agree to stop fighting, hiding, resisting because you know that you will not win or succeed.

"I'm grateful for God's grace. Without it I wouldn't have ever gotten through my addiction alive.

"I'm grateful today that God is who he says he is and that I find myself walking in his light.

"I need to remind myself of these moments. This story was the moment God put his hand on my shoulder and led me out of my own darkness."
-Nathan Pingry

(Finally, for Nathan it was for 'realsies.' Nathan is over two years sober and involved in a faith-based outreach program helping others for 'realsies.')

CREW BOSS

One of Sawyer's fellow wildland firefighters and crew boss, would observe Sawyer reading the small New Testament he always carried in his pack.

"Good Book, Grooms?" the man would jab.

"Why, yes, sir, it is in fact THE good book." Sawyer was unaffected by the mocking.

But every day Sawyer read; and everyday his friend observed—many times silently. He couldn't help but wonder about this young man who was a hard worker, loyal friend, leader and even prankster. He didn't believe all that hogwash in the Bible, as he'd call it, and didn't understand how Sawyer could. And yet, he had the greatest respect for him, as did all his co-workers. He was a leader of the first water—a man's man.

Sawyer was patient and only answered questions asked of him on their breaks—Sawyer sitting on a log, grinning up over his little New Testament.

"How d'ya know there's a God anyway," the man would snap.

"It's all in here," Sawyer would say, as he held up the Book.

"Well, I don't believe it!" the man would be emphatic, then stomp away resisting, even though down deep he knew he wanted what Sawyer had.

"I'm always here, when you're ready to talk," Sawyer would say loudly, so the man didn't miss a word.

"Ain't gonna be anytime soon!" He'd declare and then stomp away.

It was about a year later when Sawyer's friend confessed he was ready to listen. That's the day Sawyer told him about how Jesus died for his sins and offered him eternal life with Him in heaven. The man, no longer mocking, prayed and asked Jesus to save him.

He now carries his own New Testament and grins up at every newcomer that comes by and says, "Ya reading the Good Book, Boss?"

(NOTES: Getting saved is just one act, followed a bundle of long yet important words: redemption, atonement, justification, sanctification. When a person surrenders to the will of God, and sincerely asks God to save him/ her and forgive their sin, at that moment, God the Holy Spirit unites with the person's spirit never to be divided. God is one with each believer, and will never leave him/her... her/his life is transformed forever. Eternal life and the Christian journey has just begun.

Sin is any wrong doing like lying, cheating, murder, any disrespect for God or civil law, etc. There are times when people say what has become known as the sinner's prayer, but when there is no evidence of a changed life, there was no salvation. The Bible says to *'examine yourself'* to see if your salvation is genuine. There is unsurmountable danger in unbelief.)

ETHAN

Who is your closest friend, one who sticks closer than a brother? For Sawyer, it was Ethan. Partners in crime, two goofy boys (as Lilly called them); Ethan said Sawyer was daring, always excited about life; while he was the calm, smart one... Sawyer was the gas, Ethan was the brakes. They would try anything, cook anything, eat anything... all the while creating outlandish and entertaining dialogues to celebrate even the most ordinary occasions. They absolutely loved life!

And how they loved each other, were always there for each other, and loved to make music together. They would do anything for and with each other... and go the extra mile to help each other without question.

Sawyer invited his best friend to meet Christ on several occasions, but never pushed it. Sawyer's love for Ethan, his chosen brother, combined with Sawyer's faith created a knowledge in Ethan's head to the end that one day there will be a great reunion of not only believer and Savior, but also of two best friends who will share each other's company forever.

Ethan's story and his life's harmonic melody is not yet complete.

BIBLES

It was Sawyer's custom to hand out Bibles to those who were searching for meaning in their lives. Sometimes he would write a note of encouragement. This is one example of what he would write:

"Dear Brother, Joshua,
You once mentioned a seemingly unfillable pit in your
soul. I, too, have felt this pain, and through countless
trial and error, I found God. I hope one day soon you
will find Him. Hope to see you on the other side."

THE MARINE

There were so many things about the marine that Sawyer loved, admired, respected. The fact that he could get Sawyer to follow any rule at all demanded Sawyer's respect. He also gave Sawyer unconditional love, an unconditional welcome into his home and family; and eventually, his name—Grooms.

The Marine, we'll call him Ernie, accepted Sawyer, but not his God... "I don't give a @# about your God. If He was a God who loves, He wouldn't let bad things happen!" And that would be it for a while.

Over time, the marine watched Sawyer, watched his big heart, warm smile, amazing loyalty all mixed with his stupidity, flaws... and his willingness to suffer unjustly and inconveniently for others—not just friends, but people who had hurt him, people he didn't even know. The more you knew him, the more you knew you didn't know. It always made you want to know him better... he was a magnet.

Sawyer loved the marine's two sons like his own brothers. The four of them would talk trash to each other and laugh outrageously! And somewhere along the way, the marine realized how gentle Sawyer was, and couldn't hurt anyone; and when he gave you his heart, it was for real right then, right there.

Sawyer always found good in people that others didn't—saw treasure where others saw trash, and he'd stick out that big hand with that big smile. And it wasn't long before Sawyer's big heart had won the marine for the Lord. His drinking stopped, his language cleaned up and he started attending church with his family.

He once met with others around a praise fire and

held up his Bible, proclaiming its validity, "If you don't believe every word of this, you can kiss my_____!" He believed, nothing wavering.

Mrs. Marine, we'll call her Pauline, already a believer now had the husband she always dreamed of. The same man she married, just better.

Sawyer's death not only devastated his birth family, but also this family. "A part of me still expects him to walk through that door with that cheesy grin and say, 'Hey, pops.' If you've never experienced the loss of a child, I hope you never find out what that is like. I never imagined I could hurt this much and still be alive. It's a pain that never goes away."

Someone once said, 'The price of love is grief, and the price of great love is great grief.'

HOSPITALITY

"I only met your son once. The day my mom died, I was on business in Iowa and he 'took me in' like a brother. I deeply regret not being able to repay his kindness and miss his smile and courageous spirit. We'll meet again, someday, 'somewhere.'"

–James Sutterfield

LINCOLN HILL

Comments written to Sawyer's mother from inmates at Lincoln Hill prison after she took Sawyer's story to them with his permission before he died.

The story she took was about a young man who had ADD, who didn't have a father in the home for a positive role model, who had difficulty in school, and who practiced the high-risk behavior of drinking and fighting.

She added it was not unusual for people who are wired to be warriors and heroes to practice high risk behavior in order to feel relevant and worthy. Without positive options, this need may reveal itself in substance abuse and hurting others. Self-control is always more difficult, than hurting others. Many so-called friends they run with expect such high-risk behavior.

TOUCHED
A 12-yr-old victim, who was bullied, shot and beaten, still remembered it like it was yesterday. Yet, Sawyer's story touched his heart.

MOTIVATED
Others said they were going to use Sawyer's story as motivation to do better, and not let what they've done or what had happened to them bring them down or let their mistakes take control of their lives."

HOPEFUL
Some began to understand how even simple crimes can leave people emotionally scarred for life. Some said by the time they leave prison, they hoped they would also have the power to help others instead of leaving them to deal with their problems by themselves—the power to take a negative action and turn it into a positive and helpful outcome. Sawyer's story showed them that almost anything is possible if you are willing to continue to fight and struggle instead of giving up.

YOU HAVE TO EARN RESPECT
Sawyer's story proved to be a huge influence on some after they realized that no matter how many who saw him and viewed his tattoos, his long his hair, or his many scars as a sign of a man to be feared—a man who lacked character, or as some other negative; when he came into town with a fire, he was no longer looked on as a problem, but as the man who solves the problem. He earned their respect... a great tribute.

As the firefighters marched back from a fire, tired, dirty, and smelling like smoke, crowds of townspeople would gather along the streets holding thank-you signs. The people's first negative impressions changed into well-deserved respect, gratitude and admiration.

WILDLAND FIREFIGHTER'S BIBLE

A gift from his Uncle Rob, the little New Testament Sawyer carried in his line gear was given to him when he was in jail to help pass the time.

After Sawyer's death, Rob saw the need for more New Testaments... saw how many others wanted to carry them and read them. He ordered 100 copies and placed 'In Memory of Sawyer W. Grooms, Feb. 14, 1990 – May 2, 2016' stickers on the outer sleeve and inside the Bible's front cover.

Over 80 of these have been distributed to the wildland firefighters, acquaintances, and to those to whom Sawyer witnessed, or wanted to witness, with the confidence that

"My Word that goes out from my mouth:
it will not return to me empty, but will
accomplish what I desire and will achieve the
purpose for which I sent it." –Isaiah 55:11.

108

Note the red bandana, the yellow shirt,
and (where pictured) the green pants.

NOAH'S ARK
A testimony to God's protection, provision, and salvation for His people.
(Photo by M. Garrison)
Noah's Ark, pictured here, is the length of 3 football fields and is made up of 1.3 million board feet of lumber. It is a full size re-creation of the original ark, constructed on site in Williamston, Kentucky, under the direction of Ken Hamm and team.
First open to the public in 2016.

Sawyer's note on Chapter 9 may have looked like this:
"My aunt Marilyn helped me write this, as a matter of fact, she wrote nearly all of it. I only met her once in my life when I was six.
She scared me because she laughed a lot.
But I learned she never cared what others thought of her, and I loved her for that. And I knew we were kindred spirits because she loved the out-of-doors, was fearless, adventurous, musical, artist and writer. If she had only written this book before I was promoted to glory, we would've had great talks and sang harmony together."

Chapter 9

THE MEASURE OF GOD

If Sawyer had preached a sermon,
Chapter 9 would've been that sermon.
And it might've been called:
"When Sawyer changed his measure of
God, God Changed Sawyer."

"I will give you a new heart, and put a new
spirit in you... My Spirit, and will move you to
follow my decrees... and keep my laws."
–Ezekiel 36.26, 27.

"WHO ARE YOU, GOD?"

What we think of God—our perception or measure of God—dictates the tone, essence and flavor of our entire life. Also, what we think of God determines what we think of sin (pages 119, 120); what we think of sin determines what we think of others, and what we think of others determines what we think of ourselves. Ultimately, until we fully see God, we cannot fully see ourselves.

Who is God to you? What does He look like? Even without being aware of it, the one thing most of us attempt to determine about people when we first meet is whether or not we can trust them. Since only 7% of communication is through words—and if they aren't honest, they wouldn't tell us anyway—we look at their eyes, gestures, at what makes them laugh or get angry.

I picked up a Ron Comfort pamphlet at our church

that says of a young man who confessed, "I find it hard to believe everything God says in the Bible."

Comfort smiled at that, and quickly asked the man his name, to which the man answered, 'Paul.'

"I don't believe you," said Comfort. "What is your name?" he asked again.

"Paul," the young man repeated, showing his impatience at Comfort's disbelief.

"You seem a little upset, young man, because I didn't believe you."

"Right! My name IS Paul—it's my name and I should know!"

"Paul, God has set his words in perfect order in the Bible telling you His name and who He is. When you say you don't believe Him, He feels the same way. After all, they are His words and 'He should know'."

We can't physically look God in the eye and measure His honesty, but we can observe the integrity of His handiwork in nature; we can look and see that He's fulfilled every possible promise / prophecy in His Word; and we can look those in the eye who are called His children... like Sawyer, who would greet you with that big toothy grin, reach out that big hand, share his big heart and say, 'God loves you,' and you knew it was so.

So, to many of you, God looks like Sawyer...minus the human flaws.

"ISN'T GOD GOOD? MY GOD IS SO BIG!"

Sawyer's God was good—He was big. When he was very young, one of his favorite songs went like this:

My God is so big, my God is so mighty
There's nothing my God cannot do.

And often it's not until we see God for who He is, sometimes not until we reach bottom and there're no more options, are we motivated to yield 100% of ourselves to Him. Sawyer saw God in the grandeur of nature, in the grandeur and truth of the Bible, in the grandeur of faith, and in the grandeur of His love and mercy. And once he saw God, he was never the same.

The fact that God loved him and would not—did not!—abandon him was huge to Sawyer. God was a true Father who loved him and never, ever left him to figure things out on his own.

Imagine the most awesome, incredible, famous person you can think of walking into the room to sit beside you. For me, it was Rosey Greer—6' 6", 370# of muscle, Los Angeles Giants... the Fearsome Foursome. I knew he was going to speak at this charity dinner... I knew he was going to sit right beside me. But when he walked in, I turned white and nearly fainted with fear! That is just a hint of what it is like to *see* God.

Then imagine that famous person taking up residence in your home, where you can talk to him every day. It changes your focus, what you do, what you think about, and how you feel about yourself.

When Sawyer saw how big God was (bigger than the universe... all the universes), and how small he was (dust), on that day he had no choice but to humble himself—yield 100% of his will, life, heart, mind, soul, strength—before his Maker. He knew then that if he didn't trust God completely, he really didn't trust God at all. This was the day Sawyer changed his measure of God, and God changed Sawyer.

WHY WE LIMIT GOD... *"BLACK AND WHITE"*

Well...we live in a world of black and white limits: speed limits, exhaustion, doses of medications, budgets, mph, mpg, expirations, death, things that run their course, price tags, clocks, calendars, bills, seasons, capacities, measurements, only to name a few.

When we describe something, we generally speak

in limits. In the poem, *See This Land*, the author presents the irony of trying to describe the vastness of the Yukon as being so big as to be able to fit the whole world in it 'a time or two.'

And various imaginative and exciting movies about space and the future have given us just a taste—a hint—of 'limitlessness.'

God is limitless—not a concept easily understood by finite minds—minds that must deal with limits constantly. But God's power, knowledge, compassion, mercy, love, etc. are not limited. Yet, He joys in knowing us so much that He has written our names on the palms of His hand. (Is 49.16), not unlike Sawyer writing God's Word on his hands and arms. Imagine a God that writes your name on his hand to have it ever before Him because He loves you so much. That is Sawyer's God.

Our unbelief is the only thing that limits God, and our mind is the only thing that limits us. In the Bible there's a story of a man named Peter who walked on water. He was in a small boat with friends—other disciples—when the sea became stormy and wild. Jesus appeared to them walking on the water! He spoke to the angry sea and immediately the sea was calm. Then Peter (must've been a lot like Sawyer) asked to do something humanly impossible—get out of the boat and walk on the water with Jesus!! By faith, Peter did just that; but as soon as he began to doubt, he began to sink.

So what is your measure of God? Is He as big as Sawyer's God? Someone you trust with your dreams, ambitions, and future? Are you still walking on water today, or have doubts crept in causing that 'sinking feeling'?

Sawyer loved the book of Proverbs—called it the 'fortune cookie' book, because it seemed every verse was foretelling... shedding a bit more light on life. These were two of his favorite verses:

**"Trust in the Lord with all your heart, and
lean not unto your own understanding.**

"In all your ways acknowledge Him
and He will make your paths straight."
—Proverbs 3:5, 6

Sawyer never learned the months of the year.
That did not keep him from greatness.

I think of Proverbs as the eye (I) Doctor book... good for all those "I" diseases that ale us, such as sIn and prIde. Pride comes in many different flavors (so does sin): attitude, comparing, coveting, negativism, I want, I need, jealisy (I know there's no 'I' in the word, jealousy, but in reality, it is totally filled with 'I'), etc.

Prov. 13:10 says 'pride only breeds quarrels.' So, if you feel ill-at-ease with someone, you may want to look closer to see if you have any eye (I) problems.

EVERY PERSON HAS FOUR NEEDS... *"COOL STUFF"*

In the 42-year course of my teaching career, I taught a psychology class. Some highlights I will never forget are certain basics that were key in understanding the core cause of some serious problems plaguing mankind in general.

Some of the things detailed were the four needs of every human: 1) responsibility, 2) skill, 3) knowledge, and 4) acceptance. Without these, self-esteem collapses, and may result in substance abuse, poor grades, school drop outs, illegitimate pregnancy, and suicide.

How do we combine these two topics: 1) our perception of God, who created us to have communion with Him, and who will never leave us to figure out life on our own; and 2) four needs of every person.

When we believe on Jesus Christ and ask Him to save us, the Holy Spirit comes to live within us and we become a part of God's family—a child of the King. We immediately have acceptance—part of a family where we are loved and cherished... part of God's plan.

God also gives His family members gifts of skill and

Sawyer was struck by lightning once while on fire assignment; and knew the power of fire, storm and flood. Still, he found betrayal more frightening than them all.

knowledge, responsibilities, and specific tasks —there is 100% employment. We gain knowledge of God by reading the Bible, from other believers, through the Holy Spirit's leading, and through His creation.

Plus, God not only commends us for gaining knowledge of Him, but also for formal and / or hands-on education, and being diligent in whatever our hands find to do.

"...work diligently with your hands...win the respect of others..." -I Thessalonians 4:11

If you had known Sawyer, one of the gifts God assigned to him was to 'see beauty in others.' He saw treasure where many others saw trash; and he was careful to let everyone he met know they were valuable to him and to God—even though society had stamped many of them 'throw-aways.'

SIN—A MARK IS MISSED

Sin... what is it? Certainly sin is committing any of the 'thou shall not's' in the Ten Commandments. Jesus went on to say that even thinking about committing any of the 'thou shall not's' is sin; or any thought of foolishness; or to him that knows to do good and doesn't; or anything that is not of faith.

And this book isn't big enough to list everything that is sin.

Sin is simply 'not hitting the mark.' What is that mark? There are four verses that rise to the top when it comes to defining what that mark is.

"Fear God and keep His commandments; for this is the whole duty of man." -Ecclesiastes 12:13

"Love the Lord your God with all your heart... soul... strength and... mind; and love your neighbor as yourself." -Luke 10:27

"What does the Lord require of you? To act justly, love mercy and to walk humbly with your God." -Micah 6:8

"... humble yourselves... pray... seek my face... turn from your wicked ways..." -II Chronicles 7:14

For Sawyer, while God's forgiveness was instantaneous and absolute, hitting the mark was not. And though forgiveness is immediate, healing and release from the sin often takes some time.

As a bullseye shooter, I have had a lot of experience with 'hitting the mark,' and even more experience with NOT hitting the mark. Shooting bullseye targets at 50 yards is considered the most difficult accuracy sport in the world. It's like taping up a 50-cent piece at 50 yards, holding your pistol with one hand, no artificial support, and shooting that coin 10 times.

I've shot 10 100's, but never 10 x's (100 8-x is my best... so far). I've heard of people who have shot 10x.

When I shoot, I have to block out everything else because every other thing is a distraction. I've trained with the masters to absolutely focus on knowing how to make the shot—every shot—with absolute precision. I know how to, but doing it? Well... Hitting the mark demands my best, my all; and unless I practice every week, I lose my 'edge.' Practicing daily is even better.

In our walk with God—and whether or not we consider ourselves to be 'God walkers,' we will all answer to Him in the end—sin is anything that misses the mark, center of the target... doesn't hit the bullseye.

Some curious things about the eye: It has been said that the only way to stop a charging bull is to hit it in the eye; we are the apple of God's eye; our eye is one of the most vulnerable parts of our body; and when you look someone in the eye, you can see yourself.

According to the Bible, our goal as Christ followers—Christians—is to study to show ourselves approved, or to be more like Him, which is our 'mark' to hit. He was sinless. Even though I know of shooters who have shot nearly perfect scores in bullseye, I am not one of them. But every day that is my goal, the same way my goal—or mark—every day is to be more like Christ.

As a Christian, I will never be perfect—never be sinless—and God knows that. He knows 'our frame.' All He expected of Sawyer, all He expects of you or me is that we give Him our whole heart. The following song expresses what it is to give our whole heart to God.

A Sacrifice Unspotted
By M. Garrison ©2013
My heart was all God wanted, He asked no gold from me,
Nor did He ask that my heart be guilt-free;
Twas my heart with all its pain and pride
He asked for lovingly
For if He had my heart he knew He had the rest of me.

And even when I gave the Lord my heart entirely,
At times I'd take a portion back to me;
Then the Spirit came reminding
How much better it would be
If as He directs my life he had each part of me.

Blessed Lord to thee I'll cling, I surrender everything
Please except this humble offering that I bring;
Whatever, Lord, you want I'll be, rearrange until you see
A sacrifice that is unspotted in me.

GOD'S PROMISE... *"I WEIGHED MY OPTIONS"*

There's a fatal flaw in each of the following three suggestions concerning victory over sin in our lives.

1. <u>Ask God to help you hit the mark</u>. **REALITY**: You cannot overcome sin by merely adding God's help to supplement your own plans. TRUTH: Yes, pray

✗ACCEPT   119

for God's help, then humble yourself and be willing to turn from your wicked way. Until you seek Him with ALL your heart you cannot truly find His help in overcoming sin.

2. <u>Make God a part of your life.</u> **REALITY**: God doesn't want to be just a part of your life. **TRUTH**: Make God ALL your life, not just a part of it.

3. <u>You can do this if you try.</u> **REALITY**: You can't do this no matter how hard you try. **TRUTH**: You have no power to do this even if you try really, really hard, but with God you can do anything.

"I can do everything through Him (Christ) who gives me strength." -Philippians 4:13

He is the Overcomer, He is the only one who can make a way for you to turn from your sin and provide an escape plan for future sin.

Our responsibility is to put God first in our lives, His promise is that if we do that, it will change our lives.

We soon find that "Behold, your God" is seeing God as the Creator God, the Protector God, the Healer God, the victorious God, and the Forgiver God who hears and answers prayer.

Now, because of our nature, we will not be perfect in this life. But God knows that our hearts can be perfect before Him, and that's all he wants from us.

<u>Once we are saved, God sees us as sinless...</u> as sinless as Jesus Christ who died our death (the price of sin is death), paying the price of all our past sin, present sin and future sin.

Following Christ is not a faith of convenience. God says, *"Come unto me all you who are weighed down and weary." -Matthew 11:28.*

But if you are looking for the convenient, the easy way, He adds in essence in *Revelation 3:15, 16*, 'if you really don't mean it, don't come.'

120

"You're neither cold nor hot. I wish you were one or the other! Because you are lukewarm, I will spit you out of my mouth! (Loosely translated, 'You make me sick!')

If Christianity were a faith of convenience, there would've been no martyrs, no trials, no commandments, no crosses, no losses. Jesus set the example—His death on the cross wasn't convenient. It was ultimate torture, ultimate pain because He took the punishment—not for His own sin, He had none—but for every sin every person has ever or will ever commit.

One of Sawyer's many loves—photography.
"Our photo together is going to have to wait until I join you in heaven—I hope you took your camera." —AG

Abraham, for instance, was asked to sacrifice his son, Isaac (at the last moment God provided a lamb for the sacrifice); and David, armed with only a slingshot and 5 stones was asked to face off not only Goliath but 3000 experienced and armed Philistines.

Sawyer found himself under the conviction of God, a new crossroad in his life, where again he could choose the easy out, or do the right thing... convenience not even a player. He had been prepped for this day, God equipping him since birth—always swimming upstream, always thinking the easy way was illogical.

INCREDIBLE VALUE—BOUGHT WITH A PRICE

Becoming a Christian—admitting you're a sinner, knowing you cannot save yourself, and trusting Jesus to forgive your less-than-honorable ways and transform your mind and heart—is the greatest, life-changing event that could ever happen to you.

When you are saved, you become a grafted-in member of God's family, and you will always be family. There will be times you may lose your focus on God; but He is a loving Father, and will draw you back to Himself.

Ezekiel 36 and Romans chapters 1-8, walk us through the salvation experience—beginning with the initial transformation when we realize we are unable to save ourselves. When we pray and ask God to forgive us of every sin we have or will commit, to save us and strengthen us, to believe God has promised to do many things for us, we will experience what Sawyer did. (Ezekiel, Psalms and Jeremiah were some of Sawyer's favorite books in the Bible.)

"I will save you from all your uncleanness
(godless habits)... Then, you will remember
your evil ways (the sin you used to commit)
and you will loathe (hate) your sin."
-Ezekiel 36.31

Being bought with a price is like if you get caught breaking the law, and you stand in the courtroom where God, the judge, brings down the gavel, pronouncing you guilty of whatever, and tells you how much you owe.

"I can't pay that," you say in shock...

Then Jesus comes to your side and says, "I will pay that for you. Do you believe I can and will do that?"

At that moment you have a choice—to believe or don't. It could be the moment of salvation, or it could be the last time He'll make that offer and you will rot in sin's prison. Serious business.

"He came to His own people,
but they did not receive Him,
"But to everyone who did receive Him,
He empowered them to become the children of God.
–John 1:11, 12

If you have sincerely asked Jesus to save you, you have the glory of God in you now. Your body became the temple—abiding place—of the Holy Spirit since the moment that you believed and asked God to forgive you and save your soul.

Jesus came to live with, rub shoulders with, to save His people from their sin. People will fail you, shun you, look the other way; but Jesus never will. He came to save everyone. If you had been the only person on earth, He would still have come... just for you.

...just for you is what first drew Sawyer to God for 'realsies.' He was of value to his Creator... the Creator of the entire universe. And God had a plan for him to accomplish important and valuable work. He would never be abandoned, would always be loved no matter what he did, no matter the difficulties... no matter.

The four things Sawyer needed: responsibility, skill, knowledge and acceptance became reality. He was responsible before God, he was blessed with skill and knowledge of fire, music, social skills and was accepted for exactly who he was the very moment he cried out to God to not just help him, but to take him and remake him—make him stronger.

SEND OUT YOUR LIGHT... *"COURAGE TO SPEAK"*

When Sawyer was two-years old and was in church with his mom, winding his little fingers through her long, curly hair, he listened intently to this new pulpit-pounding preacher.

When the preacher inserted a dramatic pause to let his last point settle in to his listeners, Sawyer saw it as an opportunity to speak his mind. "THAT man has a bad attitude," His child's mind simplifying the gesture.

Folks nearby gasped and giggled. The preacher cleared his throat and regrouped. He finished a little ahead

Funeral display.

of schedule, and made a beeline for the two when he ended... said that he did not appreciate that outburst.

"You know it was not meant with disrespect, Pastor," Myra apologized, "but Sawyer's been taught not to pound things or yell when he's upset. And when he does, I tell him it's because he's got a bad attitude."

"Well, I don't have a bad attitude," he said in his defense, "and I would appreciate it if you would teach this child to be silent in church."

Needless to say, we sought out a more understanding, and more forgiving church.

From childhood, Sawyer shared the Gospel—Good News of Christ; souls were saved, lives were changed. Blah, blah, blah... he had read it all, heard all the sermons (slept through most); but now there was something different... something exciting... interesting... something powerful. He used to share 'a Jesus' he had read about; now he shared THE Jesus he had seen. He had a heart after the missionary, C.T. Studd, who said: "Some want to live within the sound of church and chapel bell... I want to run a rescue shop within a yard from hell."

Sawyer was now running after God—God had not changed... it was Sawyer's perception of God that had changed. Jesus Christ has always been the perfect radiance of heaven (brighter than the sun!), the absolute fullness of boundless love, mercy and unending fathomless grace (God's riches at Christ's expense).

When we find ourselves face-to-face with Almighty God, our Maker, like Joshua, our only choice is to humble ourselves, fall on our faces, abhor all our sin... and turn white with fear at how great God is and what dust we are.

BUCKETS OF MERCY
(from the song, Mercy Buckets, by Patterson Hood)
If you woke up on the wrong side of the bed,
count on me.
If you're feeling that freight train

running through your head, count on me.
If you just need a friend to talk to,
or maybe not talk at all.
I will bring you buckets of mercy...

COMPLETE IN THEE
(from the song by Aaron R. Wolfe 1850)
Complete in Thee! no work of mine
Can take, dear Lord, the place of Thine;
Your blood has pardon bought for me,
And I am now complete in Thee.

18 INCHES... *"NOT ACTUALLY BELIEVING"*

It's been said the difference between heaven and hell is 18 inches—the distance from one's head to one's heart. We must believe with ALL our heart that Jesus is able to pay the price and save us completely.

**"For it is with your heart that you believe
and are justified, and it is with your mouth
that you confess (Jesus) and are saved."
–Romans 10:10**

You see, the demons also believe (with the head) and fear. But a head knowledge will never save... faith has to be rooted in the heart. The demons are not followers of Christ, nor will they ever be.

**"You believe that there is one God? Good!
Even the demons believe that and shudder."
–James 2:19**

You can tell the difference between a head and a heart belief by whether or not you continue in and are drawn to things of God. If all you did was pray some words without faith, and have no life change—no works—God sends you and others a warning:

126

"Small is the gate and narrow is the road that leads to life, and only a few find it... by their fruit you will recognize them. Not everyone who says to me, 'Lord, Lord' will enter the kingdom of heaven...
–Matthew 7:14, 15, 20, 21

We rub shoulders every day with those who think / assume they're saved because they've repeated a prayer, or attend church. Truth is, once you're saved you will be different than you were before. Truly, after this life, we will be surprised by those we see in heaven, and by those we don't. There is a life in heaven to gain and a death in hell to escape.

HOLY WAR... *"UNABLE TO WIN BY STRENGTH ALONE"*

At the moment of salvation—when you trust Jesus with your life—you step into a war. You and God are on one side, your three enemies are on the other side. Their names are 1) the devil, 2) the world, and 3) your own flesh—lust of the eyes, lust of the flesh and pride of life. The devil is a thief who comes to steal your faith and to destroy you (John 10:10). The 'world' in this context, refers to the anti-God worldly system that loves darkness rather than light (John 3:20). Your needy flesh has desires, and is never satisfied. If left to itself, it will meet those needs by indulging in things that are sinful, but pleasant; detestable, yet comforting; temporary, yet satisfying. Your flesh cries continually, 'Feed me!'

Sometimes temptations seem relentless, returning again and again like a bad headache. Everyone is tempted, but not of God. We're led astray by our own lusts; and, of course, satan knows when we are weak, and just how to tempt us!

Our former pastor, Mark Dickerson Sr, would say you can't help it if a wrong thought crosses your mind any more than you can stop birds from flying over your head.

But you don't have to think that second thought, any more than you don't have to let those birds make a nest in your hair! The second thought is a choice.

James 2:14, 15 lists the steps to sin: **lust** - we see something we want; **temptation** - we reason, 'why not?'; **enticement** - like a fishing lure, we can't stop thinking about it; **sin** - we run after it and take the bait—hook line and sinker; **'death,'**—sin leaves us ineffective, without the ability to think clearly, sometimes causing us to be sin's slave for years! Thank God He has promised a way to escape so we can be freed from the strangling, seemingly unbreakable grip of sin and its addictions.

Sawyer saw ideas, ideals—practically everything—through a different lens. He described sin as the dark move in life, or a move towards darkness. Yet, though it seemed mysterious, fun, thrilling, adventurous, exciting and challenging, in the end, he saw how those dark moves brought chaos, loss, death and destruction.

He also saw sin as 'missing the mark.' Throughout history, for instance, an archer practices so his arrow will hit the mark. In battle, intentionally missing the mark would have the same result as sin has in our lives— loss in battle, maybe captivity... maybe death.

So, if after I'm saved, sin no longer has any power over me, why do I keep sinning!? I heard an example in a sermon by Dr. Jim Shettler that makes sense of this in one picture: When we are saved, we are made alive in Christ and our bodies are dead to sin. We are enabled by the Holy Spirit to live a Godly Christian life, no longer surrendering our bodies to serve sin.

After that, any urge to sin—worry, discouragement, fear, doubt, etc—in our flesh is a phantom pain, much like what someone who has lost an arm or leg would sense. (Anyone who has experienced phantom pain will tell you that real or not, your brain tells you that you are in pain.) But just as that missing limb is dead, so your old sinful nature is dead and you don't have to feed it.

Sawyer would tell you from his own experiences that God is able to turn off the pain of sin in the blink of an eye. Prayer and believing that God will do what He said He would, will cause sin's confining but imaginary walls to evaporate. When sin is chasing you, and you can feel its hot breath on the back of your neck, run like hell is chasing you, because it is.

"If my people will humble themselves, pray, turn from their sin; then will I hear, forgive, heal..." –II Chronicles 7:14. Life for the believer is all-out war, not a game. It's won or lost on the unseen spiritual battlefields of the mind.

*"Though you used to be slaves to sin...
you have been set free." —Rom.6:14*

Uncle Rob wears the Wildland Firefighter Foundation tee, "Compassion Spreads Like Wildfire." Yes, it does!

Dr. Jim Shettler also painted a picture about living a victorious Christian life by the power of God and not trying to do it in our own strength. It's like the little child whose dad told him to blow grass clippings off the paved drive. Dad checks on the child after a few minutes and finds the child down on hands and knees, mouth close to the pavement huffing a puffing. Dad smiles, and gets the leaf blower he left nearby. He shows the child how much easier the job is when you use power.

Jesus zeroed in one sin we sometimes fail to see—the sin of pride. In Luke 18.10, we find the prayers of two men: the religious 'Pharisee' (a church member in good standing, seemingly perfect in every way), and the poor 'publican' (tax collector—a basic laborer).

First, when the Pharisee went forward to pray, he looked up saying, "God, I thank you that I am not like other men—extortionists, unjust, adulterers, or even as this tax collector;" then went on to list his good works.

(I didn't know I was being a Pharisee, until I noticed when I became aware of sin in others, the first thing I thought of was how God was going to punish them. The Holy Spirit's dealing with me was specific in that I am not their judge; but rather, I am to pray for them and love them as Jesus would and have compassion on them.)

When the tax collector got up to pray, he didn't dare lift up his eyes but smote his breast saying, "God be merciful to me a (the) sinner, and 'cleanse me by your atoning blood.'"

Jesus said, "I tell you, this man went down to his house justified, rather than the other."

"Everyone who exalts himself will be humbled, and he who humbles himself will be exalted." -Luke 18.14

Yes, we do sin after we are saved, and can lose the joy of our salvation; but we cannot lose our salvation. Even though our sin makes God sad, He waits for us to repent and turn from that sin just as the prodigal son's father watched and waited every day for his son to come home. And, oh, what joy there was when he did.

> *"Restore to me the joy of your salvation."*
> *–Psalm 51:12*

In his last year, Sawyer refused to settle for anything less than the joy of the Lord. He kept his eyes on Christ, and didn't look back. Like Sawyer, we need to focus on the greatness and faithfulness of Jesus. How big our faith is doesn't matter, (faith the size of a mustard seed can move a mountain!) but the object of our faith absolutely matters.

One evening after Sawyer had been drinking, he asked him mother, "Do you know why I'm tattooed... why I dress the way I do... wear my hair the way I do?"

She confessed she didn't think there was a particular reason.

"It's so people will think twice before they try to hurt me," he confessed, revealing his physical fear.

An old song from the 90's, with its plaintive words and soulful sound, makes a person look inside himself to see his own sadness and fear: *"Did you ever feel the pain that He felt upon the cross... Blinded by rainbows, watching the wind blow... do you hide away the fear... do you dream at night..." (Blinded by Rainbows, Rolling Stones, 1994).*

Sawyer, too, feared this loneliness of abandonment and betrayal—and considered these far more hurtful than any physical pain. In spite of this, he knew his relationship with his heavenly Father was for *'realsies'* and forever, confident that God would never, never abandon him.

> *"Never will I leave, (or) abandon you."*

Sawyer recognized the need for constant vigilance, because old fears did still creep back in... especially in his weakest and loneliest moments.

Pastor Kris, however, suggests when satan comes reminding us of our past, we should remind him of his future. With Jesus we have already won the war!

The loving and loyal support of a mother, brothers, aunts, uncles, grandparents, second parents, Ernie and Pauline, Lilly, Ethan, his firefighter family who weren't about to bail on him were all important.

Still the heart of each person was created to know God, and cannot truly rest until it is in a relationship with its Creator. We all have a longing to know Him who knows us better than we know ourselves, the One who holds the future and the One who has already written the beginning and the ending.

Above: Beautiful Wisconsin sunrise.
Right: Sawyer with chain saw and Uncle
Rob. Sawyer was a master with the saw.

"You will keep him in perfect peace whose mind is steadfast because he trusts in you." –Isaiah 26:3

When Sawyer got his God relationship right, all his other relationships started falling into place, and the more he let go and let God, the more his fear began to decrease, and his peace began to increase. He could tell you that God is able to turn off the power of that dark, relentless, pulling sin in a heartbeat.

Our measure of God makes or breaks the rest of our life. Ephesians 6 says the only way to be victorious over satan, sin and fear is to protect ourselves with the complete armor of God (each of which is Jesus Christ): 1) Truth; 2) Righteousness; 3) Peace; 4) Faith; 5) Salvation; and 6) the Word of God.

Jesus Christ and Him alone—not Him plus other beliefs or religious practices—He is the One who is able to protect you, deliver you, save you, empower you, strengthen you, show you how to hit the 'mark,' bring you out of darkness to the light and set you free.

Jesus Christ alone.

"Always Remember..."
Sawyer William Grooms – Firefighter, Friend.

PART 3
ALWAYS REMEMBER

Sawyer loved the ice caves.

"Thanks to the ice caves, there's no off season for Cornucopia this year
by Hope McLeod, Staff Writer, Bayfield County Journal 12/2012 (excerpt)
CORNUCOPIA --The Western Gateway to the Apostle Islands
National Lakeshore (AINL) and the closest town to the sea caves,
Cornucopia has recently become a pit stop for thousands turning
off Highway13 in search of basic amenities. Do the math: resident
population 100; ice cave population since January, 76,000.
"After the first weekend of shell-shock, we kind of rallied and put everything
together," said Kevin Hunt, owner of Star North, the only gas station and
convenience store in Corny. "And we've been taking care of business ever since."

Chapter 10

THE MOSAIC, THE MILESTONES, THE MARK HE LEFT

THE MOSAIC
WHAT MAKES THE MAN?

Parts of man—the physical, intellectual, emotional, spiritual; a man's fears, dreams, accomplishments, ability to laugh, passion, priorities, family—all these woven together become the person we recognize and revere, or dread and detest, all to some degree.

If we were to answer the question, 'What made *this* man?' We could say genetics. He was a large, handsome man, a deep thinker, with a need for human bonding, strong, musical, a dream chaser with a thirst for adventure. And we could say environment. The people closest to him instilled compassion, confidence, values, work ethic, a love for God... and a fear of being alone.

One of the most defining parts of a man is where he has drawn the line in the sand—the line he will not cross, the essence and culmination of his values. This may or may not be the most memorable mark a man leaves behind when he's gone, but often is.

Each of us can think about where we've drawn our own line, and even write down our intentions. Yet, without integrity, life can quickly muddy that line.

So, where did Sawyer draw the line? Others saw it in everything he did. Others are the best gage when it comes to defining exactly where we have laid it down, whether or not it ever moves, and what moves it.

Then there's the 'how' of the man. Adjectives like diligent, which describes the presence of tenacity—he never gave up; consistent, which describes the quality of integrity—the same throughout; unselfish... love—putting the needs of others before his own; thoughtful, the quality of compassion—putting love in action; and encouraging, the quality that inspires... gives hope... boosts your spirit... raises you up.

THE MILESTONES – HE ACCOMPLISHED MUCH

As a firefighter...
"He was extremely skilled as a wildland firefighter and by all accounts very well-liked and respected by those he worked beside. The hard work he did helped further the mission of the Bureau of Indian Affairs of protecting and improving Indian Trust Lands. In addition, he helped to protect and improve tens of thousands of acres of forests and wildlands across our entire nation."

As a musician...
Sawyer and Ethan performed over 75 concerts in their five years as a band; everywhere from Wisconsin to Texas to Los Angeles. Whether it was one or 1000 listeners, Sawyer didn't care—he loved the music. HE embodied the soul, sound, rhythm, and energy of the music.

*"I can still hear his baritone voice
singing full throttle."*

*"I was blessed to have had the chance to make music
with this guy—he made you play from the heart."*

"He made and played songs like they were his last."

"I chose to play." —SWG

His laughter...
"He was a great storyteller—the kind that could get everybody laughing—and laughter brings people together."

His Passion...
"You lived life to the fullest! It's not how much you did, but how you did it!"

His priorities...
His priorities included God, family, Lilly (Baluga), friends, firefighting, music, adventures, being out-of-doors, cats, whitefish livers, pranks, swimming upstream, inspiration, inventions.

"He was never too busy to care about someone else."

His time...
"He spoke seven words to me, 'Don't ever stop, don't ever give up!' He was never lazy and didn't let opportunities lapse. That wasn't who he was."

THE MARK HE LEFT – HEALER
"I am going to use Sawyer's story as motivation to do better, and not let what I've done or what has happened to me bring me down. I am not what I did, I am better than that. I refuse to let my mistakes take control of my life."

REVERED
"With a heavy heart and sick stomach I am letting you know we lost an Awesome Firefighter; on the morning of May 2, Sawyer Grooms passed away at the age of 26. Sawyer became a firefighter at the age of 19 and worked with us here at Great Lakes Agency since. Many of you have worked with him and know what a beautiful, kind, humorous, talented man he was. He always had a swagger about him that screamed Awesomeness! This spring, five others and myself had been traveling and doing RX burns with him at Shakopee, Ho-Chunk, Prairie Island, Upper Sioux, Lower

Sioux, Sac and Fox, Menominee, Lac Courte Oreilles tribes. I have set up a shared photo album for people to post and view photos. https://goo.gl/photos/rDkLGcjGcKECEMrC6. PEACE AND KINDNESS TO ALL." –Dave Pergolski, Fire and Fuels Manager, BIA, Great Lakes Agency.

OPEN BOOK
"He wasn't sinless... never claimed to be.
His life was a refreshing open book."

"All gave some...
Some gave all."

Chapter 11

THE MEMORIES

THE MEMORABLE STORIES

"We met in Bayfield elementary, becoming best friends
almost immediately, causing a ruckus in class.
Both of us transferred to Washburn around the same
time and made life-long friendships along the way.
He got me to run cross country
even though I wasn't a fan of running.
We made stupid, funny home videos
of us doing dumb things kids do.
How I wish we could still do that."
-Daniel Grooms

"I remember a time when he called stating that his car
kept overheating and he and Lilly were stuck on the side
of the road by the cemetery. Pauline and I get round
the corner on our way to help, and what do we see??
His little beat up Subaru with a FULL SIZE pool table
strapped to the top!! Whaaaat?? Pauline asks him, "does
your mother know about this"? That big cheesy grin
shined bright as he simply said.... "no, it's a surprise"!!"
-Ernie Grooms

"I will never forget our times together in the
woods digging holes to China and playing pirates.
I love you and miss you already!" -Karen Tolly

"I remember you as a little kid, moving into the white house at Little Sand Bay and finding out that you were reading the same Hardy Boys books that I once did. I remember so many days in the office with your mom shaking her head as she related whatever school prank had most recently brought her a phone call from the principal, and all of us cracking up in admiration for your creativity."
–Bob Mackreth

"I remember once in 6th grade, you got in trouble for switching the 'morning prayer' cassette with Dr. Dimento. You were always doing things all of us wanted to do, but were never brave enough to do."
–Lauren Ragnier

"We loved how he would just walk in without notice and be right at home with us." –Jessica Richardson

"I remember that time we penguin-wrestled on Halloween and I split my eyebrow open. That scar on my forehead will forever be an honor." —Megan Elizabeth

HERO
"The days of heroes are not gone." –M. Foster

"I'll never be able to thank him enough for what he did for me." –Jean Williams

"Every day I got to spend with Sawyer Grooms was a lucky day." –Dave Pergolski

UNFORGETTABLE
"I only met your son once. The day my mom died, I was on business in Iowa and he took me in like a brother. I deeply regret not being able to repay his kindness and miss his smile and courageous spirit. We'll meet again, someday, somewhere." –James Sutterfield

ENCOURAGER

"Today was the hardest I've had to get through in a very long time. I didn't think it would make me break down the hardest. But somehow, some way—his way— he made us all smile in the end." -Derek Bonney

"Friends saw him as loving and loyal to the bone. When they were down, he went far out of his way to bring them up again. He could always put you in a good mood, even if he wasn't." -M. Foster

"When I started to worry about people's negative comments, he would always say, 'Who cares what anybody else thinks, just be yourself." -M. Foster

"He gave me something I often lose—hope." -D. Bonney

PRESENCE

"The world lost an amazing man today. His heart was so big, his laugh so outrageous, his talent so profound."-M. Elizabeth

"He was a lot—miss him a lot." -Hope McLeod

"He was like a son or younger brother. He'll always be with me...mind, body, spirit." -D. Pergolski

"The more you knew him, the more you knew you didn't know. It always made you want to know him better... he was a magnet." -E. Grooms

"He was a fireball, destined to burn brightly and quickly." -Bruce Purcell

"He never cared what people thought, he was never afraid to be himself." -E. Grooms

"He suited up for baseball, and then put on flip-flops! He marched to his own drum." -Pauline Grooms

"He had style, always saw the best in people and never worried when it came to other people's negative thoughts about him. He was truly a one-of-a-kind individual." -P. Christiansen

"He was always swimming upstream." -E. Grooms

"Sawyer was not the first to give much, but he did it with such flair, such humility, such honesty, such fullness, such vibrance, that once you met him, even briefly, you would never forget him." -M. Garrison

"He saw the world through a different lens." —M. Foster

LOVING
"When he gave you his heart, it was for real right then, right there." -E. Grooms

"Sawyer was always brutally honest and full of love. He brought me out of some pretty dark places just by being there."—Clarence Pratt

"Most of all, he loved the one woman who stole his heart from age eight—the unstoppable Lilly. Lilly, the game warden's daughter, she could out shoot him and give him a run for his money in countless ways; but she also supported him, loved him and saw his brilliance and shining goodness." -M. Foster

"He loved and made everyone around him feel they were worth something." -E. Grooms

"Because of Sawyer I'm forever blessed and changed." -Paula Christiansen

INSPIRATION
"He spoke seven words to me, 'Don't ever stop, don't ever give up!' He was never lazy and didn't let opportunities lapse. That wasn't who he was."
-D. Bonney

"So many have said, 'Sawyer inspired me.' Inspire means to breathe life into—and so he did." —M. Foster

"Sawyer, my friend, I threw away the chains of addiction—1 year. Forever grateful." -Nathan Pingry

"My life changed the moment I met you. I'm so thankful I got to spend time with you." -M. Elizabeth

"Thanks for being such an inspiration to me."
-Eric Strieter

"He could light a fire in you to love him, be angry with him, be inspired by him. He was a fire in us all."
—B. Purcell

NON-JUDGMENTAL
"He loved more and judged less." -P. Grooms

"He was more heart and less attack." -Melissa Grooms

FIREFIGHTER
"Awesome firefighter! Awesome friend!" -Ron Waukau

"When he was sober and on fire (on duty), he sat with his buddies he loved, but wouldn't drink— he just ate pie and coffee." -M. Foster

"He loved the rugged trail, loved carrying a 45-pound pack plus a chain saw and drip torch, and he loved sleeping outside in a tent or just under the stars."
-M. Foster

"Best crew I've been out with ever by far and it was you Sawyer, it was you that made it rock." -EP

"He was extremely skilled as a wildland firefighter and by all accounts very well-liked and respected by those he worked beside. "-Dave Pergolski

"To a great friend and firefighter, thank you for all you have done in the fire services. Your talents on the line and in life will not be forgotten... til we meet again."
—Jeremy Erickson

"His heart was so warm, he never got cold—not even when it was 2 degrees outside." -D. Pergolski

"You reached out to me and told me how us firefighters stick together. The last thing you said to me was, 'Take care, lady, talk to you later." -Jenna Lindquist

"Tragically, we lost a great guy today. Have some great memories of wild fires and deep conversations. Jam while you can." -Gordon Robertson

"Honor." -Guy Ishpeming Migizii Defoe

MUSICIAN / SINGER
"I was blessed to have had the chance to make music with this guy—he made you play from the heart."
-D. Pergolski

"I'm honored to have shared the stage with him."
—Rosendo Rowdy Perez

"I can still hear his baritone voice singing full throttle."
—Colleen Marie

"He made and played songs like they were his last."
—Bazile Panek

"May your life's song forever be sung."
—E. Strieter

"Super talented—couldn't keep an instrument away from him. He was one of the most talented artists I've ever come across." -Caitlin Haycock

"His music was amazing! He was amazing!"
—Erin Marie Thickpenny

"His memory will live on through his music and memories of all his friends and family." -Hayley Bahr

"You were one of the greatest people I know. Your music and memories will always be a part of my life." -N. Pingry

"You were an amazing artist. You will be missed."
—Christine L. Silvernail

STORYTELLER
"He was a great storyteller—the kind that could get everybody laughing—and laughter brings people together." -EP

DREAM-CHASER
"Many have shared they can't imagine life without that smile, that sense of humor and that thirst for adventure. He always chased his dream despite anything." -M.Foster

"He followed his dream regardless how of many told him it was a 'waste of time.'" -E. Grooms

TEACHER
"He accepted people as they are, but longed for them to change for the better, and grow from their mistakes into a better version of who they were." -M. Foster

"He was the best!" -D. Grooms

FRIEND
"Thanks for being a true friend." -J. Lindquist

"I feel so lucky to have been able to call him 'friend'."
-Hayley Bahr

"Thank you for being such a great friend
and true inspiration." -Jishua Hunter

HUMBLE, COMPASSIONATE, SELFLESS
"I was absolutely amazed at the number of lives he
touched, but not surprised. He was never too busy
or too far away to look you up."
-J. Erickson

"He was always early, gave away his last candy bar
and took the hardest jobs." -M. Foster

A GOOD MAN
"I hope the angels know what they have." -C. Marie

"I consider that our present sufferings are not worth
comparing to the glory that will be revealed in us."
—J. Garrison

"When the smoke clears, we will see him
in the heavenlies." -P. Grooms

"Grateful for something much greater than this life."
—E. Arnao

"I remember you as a child reading the same
Hardy Boys books I once did. Then I looked
away and you became a man. The world will be
a poorer place without you." —B. Mackreth

*Firefighters, COs and others from the USA and Canada
gather to pay tribute to their fallen brother.
(Photo by Lynn Adams.)*

*The pool table on the Subaru with a dead water pump.
The table was given half the garage and provided many hours
of fun for friends he would always invite to the house.*

That he was an outdoors guy is an understatement.

SAWYER W. GROOMS
WILDLAND FIREFIGHTER
FEB. 14, 1990–MAY 2, 2016

At Rest.

"A really good guy, and genuine individual. He had qualities you don't often see anymore."
-R. R. Perez

"People knew Sawyer—they knew he was not ordinary." -M. Foster

"The world was a brighter place with you in it."
-Kris Tribbett

"He saw something good in people others didn't."
-E. Grooms

"You were loved by many." -Julie Shevy

"His talent made an impact on many. Instant brotherhood!" -E. Grooms

INVENTOR
"He's probably already gotten David to amplify the harp." -M. Foster

DEFENDER
"He questioned everything, didn't understand the rules, stood up for the underdog and loved those that were bullied and teased." -M. Foster

HANDSOME
"You couldn't help but appreciate how handsome this man was; that and his smooth baritone voice made it almost unfair." -D. Bonney

"Sawyer was a beautiful, beautiful man, but never wielded that beauty in an arrogant way. Got mud on it, strapped big black boots on it, put frumpy clothes on it."
-H. McLeod

BROTHER
"When he used to get too drunk to drive home, it was my job to go get him and walk him home. I never thought of it as 'unfair'... he was my brother."
—Denzer

"When we were little, we were just annoyances. When we got older, he took pride in being brothers."
—D. Foster, B. Foster

"An honor to call you brother." —Ethan Hyde

"He was like a son or younger brother. He'll always be with me...mind, body, spirit." -D. Pergolski

"My homie." -Murt Greengrass

"Bridger and Sawyer shared a love for music and comedy that often walks with 'serious thinking.' Sawyer left his plastic dashboard Jesus to Bridger—a treasure."—MF

"I am forever thankful for Ernie and Pauline who gave my son their name, Grooms, and gave him extended family and great love." -Myra

"And we'd do it all over again! Thank you!" —Pauline

SOUL WINNER
"He will stand before the Father having declared the Son before men, an honor not due many of us."
-J. Garrison

CONVERSATION SNIPS
"He shared Christ with me..."
"I accepted Christ as my savior..."
"My life was changed..."

"I'm no longer on drugs..."
"I haven't had a drink in over a year..."
"I know I need to accept Christ..."
"Now I'm in a Bible study every week..."
"He came to see me in person..."
"He came to see me in prison..."
"He took time for me..."
"He gave me a Bible..."
"He was no angel, but he was righteous..."
"If he knew you were hurting, he might show
up on your doorstep... maybe at midnight."

"I will never forget Sawyer Grooms, my old roommate,
and how he was always saying that God loved me, and
cared about me. How He would give me the strength I
needed to change my life. And I will never forget
being on my knees in that jail cell. It was the moment
God put his hand on my shoulder and led me out
of my own darkness." -N. Pingry

THOUGHTFUL, GENEROUS
"He was never too busy to care about someone else."
-Adam Garrison

"It was never about how much he could get,
but how much he could give. He was physically strong,
but wouldn't hurt anyone; He gave away everything
he had, yet what he had was priceless;
he emptied himself for others, but was
the fullest man you could know."
-M. Garrison

"When he wasn't on fire, Sawyer went to church
as often as he could. He would say, 'Pray for me,
pastor,' to which the pastor would say, I will,
and will you pray for me?!'"
—M. Foster

PAIN OF PARTING

"I love you, brother. Til we meet again." -M. Elizabeth

"Words cannot be said to take away the
pain of your passing." -Matt Gordon

"I watched a video of a young woman where she
explained why she was letting her hair turn grey instead
of coloring it. Her response was beautiful. Her life
expectancy was much earlier than most, and she saw
it as a way of growing old with someone she loved. So,
in a sad yet beautiful way, Sawyer, we got to grow old
together. I love you and miss you so much every day.
Love, Beluga." —Lilly Duffy

"My heart will ever ache thinking about him."
-D. Pergolski

"One-of-a-kind. We miss you!" -P. Grooms

"I will miss you every day for the rest of my life.
You were and will always be my brother." -D. Grooms

"The world lost an amazing man today." -M. Grooms

"The world lost another great person today.
He will be greatly missed." -H. Bahr

"When will we breathe without pain? Never, that's when."
—M. Foster

"Why are the good ones always taken? I love you,
brother. Your legacy will not be forgotten." -Greg Smith

"Our photo together will have to wait until I join you
in heaven. Hope you took your camera." -A. Garrison

"Good times...sure gonna miss you, bud." -M. Greengrass

"Love you and miss you, brother." -D. Pergolski

"May 2, 2016 left a hole in my heart, don't know what I'll do without him. Not sure if it will ever heal." -A. Hyde

"I miss you, Sawyer Grooms. My heart cries,
'come back, come back!" -Ardi Foster

"I know I'll see you again, my boy. I know he knows we love him and miss him bunches! Our beautiful Sawyer!"
"My heart hurts every day."
-P. Grooms

"You will be forever missed." -P. Christiansen

"Miss you... think of you every day." -K. Tolly

"We miss you so much." -P. Grooms

"R.I.P., brother... you will be greatly missed."
-C. Haycock

"You are missed every day, brother." -D. Bonney

"R.I.P. to a well-respected, funny guy. Fly
high, my friend." -Curtis Wayka

"It feels like everything good is missing since you left."
—C. Marie

"We will always keep you in our memories and in
our hearts." —A. Hyde

"I know you're sitting on a porch swing playing guitar
in your heavenly spot. Til I see you on the other side."
"We never say goodbye, just let me hold the light;
promise that I'll see you, beyond the walls of time."
-J. Erickson

"I remember you as a little kid, then I looked away and you turned into a grown man, and a rock & roller after my own heart. And now that heart is breaking. The world will be a poorer place without you." -B. Mackreth

TRIBUTES
"I am so blessed to have been a part of your life."
—Ruth McCollough

"May the road rise up to meet you,
May the wind be always at your back,
May the sun shine warm upon your face,
And rain fall soft upon your fields.
May God hold you in the palm of His hand
until we meet again." -J. Erickson

"Listening to him play while the fire danced and the stars lit the sky on the lake—there's nothing I miss more. It's impossible for me to describe how much that moment meant to me. As the wind blows and the fire dances... I will have a fire on the beach every year and play for you this time. Love you, brother, R.I.P." -D. Bonney

"Two ways to look at time, forward and backward. What is seen is temporary, what is not seen is eternal."
-Mel Harness

"There were bald eagles everywhere today,
a fitting tribute to my pal. I know you were
there flying with them." -K. Tribbett

"If I could make days last forever,
If words could make wishes come true;
I'd save every day like a treasure
And again I would spend them with you." -M. Foster

"No one knows where you are, or how near or far
you are. Shine on, you crazy diamond!" -E. Arnao

"Each time the snow falls, I see the sparkle in your brown eyes—full of mischief and magic. Thankful you are my son forever." -M. Foster

"I've been through the fire, I've been through the flood, I've reached for the stars, I've slugged through the mud; Sometimes I was righteous, sometimes I was wrong... Speech rising in darkness has woven this song. Gone are the demons that clung to my soul! Wrongs are made right, and halves are made whole; I see you so clearly! I miss you, my friends... Look up, hear my laughter... reach out, touch my hand."
—Warrior

The Rhododendron Song
(Portions of the State song of W.V.)
(Grandma would sing this to Sawyer)
I want to climb up on that mountain!
Sing my songs to a world below
Where the Lord is e'er so near me,
when I'm breathing He can hear me...
I want to wander through the wildwood
Where the fragrant breezes blow,
Drifting back up to the mountains
Where the Rhododendrons grow.

"He was an inspiration and an amazing musician—my last message to him was, 'I'll catch up with you next time. Now it's all too real—there won't always be a next time." —Bud Summers

"Never forgotten." -A. Foster

WORDS FROM SAWYER

"Isn't God good!?" -SWG

"I want to live so the women in my life are proud of me." -SWG

"When I grow up, I want to be a fireman, pirate or rock star." -SWG

"Nemo vi vest qui mundum non." "A man is not a man who does not make the world better."

"Worry is satan's bait pile." -SWG

"When you are hopeless, everything seduces you." -SWG

"Calm waters do not make good sailors."

"Comfort breeds weakness."

"If you happen to...remember things differently, feel free to re-write your version in the 'note section' in the back of this book." -SWG

THOUGHTS OF OTHERS

"You can tell the greatness of a man by what makes him angry." -Abraham Lincoln

"Worry doesn't empty tomorrow of its sorrow, it empties today of its strength." —Corrie Ten Boom

"Bravery is courage without boundaries." -*Warrior*

"Our unbelief is the only thing that limits God, and our mind is the only thing that limits us." -*Warrior*

"Death will always come as some surprise."
-A Passion for Poetry

"Death is a memory no one can heal,
Love is a memory no one can steal."
-On an Irish Tombstone

"The nicest place to be is in somebody's thoughts;
The best place to be is in somebody's prayers;
The safest place to be is in the hands of God."
—Old Irish Proverb

"If you want things to change... become the
change, leaving footprints for others to follow."
—Warrior

"Don't try to be perfect, be brave."
*—Jennifer Rabuck (Zone Fire Mgt.
Officer, US Forest Service)*

POST SCRIPT

Ethen and his wife just had their first son and
named him Odin Sawyer.

Jeremy recently married. The ceremony
included a tribute to Sawyer.

Epilogue

THE CONCLUSION

Sawyer chose to do a lot of good in his life, but only one choice mattered when he died, "What did he do with Jesus?" And we all will make this choice. Even those who have no interest in making this choice make it by default... know God or no God. As Sawyer would say, "Are you ready to believe on Jesus for 'realsies'?

In Chapter 8, Nathan, who prayed the sinner's prayer in his jail cell, described getting saved like this. "I didn't know what getting saved looked like at first, but... to surrender is to agree to stop fighting, hiding, resisting, etc.; and you can only surrender when you realize you cannot win or succeed without Him (Jesus)."

So, this book is not just an account of the past, but also of the future. It is Sawyer's voice encouraging those who have not yet believed on Jesus, to consider His loving invitation to believe, be saved and be healed.

When Sawyer trusted in Jesus, not only was he given the gift of eternal life in heaven, but by yielding his will to God's will, he was given the power to defeat the demons that plagued him in this life.

Everyone who knew him saw the difference in his last year when he totally let go of his will and completely trusted in God alone. And when you 'let go and let God,' there will be a difference in your life, too.

"I found God. I hope one day soon you will find Him. Hope to see you on the other side." –Sawyer

Immediately after Sawyer's last breath on earth, he took his first breath in heaven face-to-face with his Savior and friend, Jesus Christ. "Isn't God Great?!"

"...away from the body... at home with the Lord."
–II Corinthians 5:8

THE BLESSING

"May the Lord bless you and keep you
and make His face shine upon you
and be gracious unto you.
May the Lord lift up His countenance upon you
and give you peace." –Numbers 6:24-26

"Just stepping on shore, and finding it heaven,
Just touching a hand, and finding it God;
Just breathing new air and finding it celestial...
Just waking up in glory...and finding it home."
—from the song Finally Home by L.E. Singer and Don Wyrtzen.

AUTHOR PAGE

Myra Foster, degreed in Archeology, was born and raised in Michigan, and has served in the National Park Service for her entire career, working in Big South Fork National River Recreation Area, TN; Buffalo River National Park, Arkansas; Grand Portage National Monument, Grand Marais, MN; and is currently the Chief of Interpretation and Education for the Apostle Lakeshore, Bayfield, WI.

She has taught numerous classes for local colleges and the National Park Service, one of which is *Elements of Personal Safety.*

She is the mother of three sons, and has published one children's book, Wilderness Tails, a coloring book with poetry to share (1993). Ms. Foster is also the 1993 recipient of the Southwest Regional Freeman Tilden Award.

Ms. Foster did the research, photos, editing and facilitating.

Marilyn (Foster) Garrison, sister to Myra's father, also born and raised in Michigan, is a retired high-school fine arts teacher of 42 years, with degrees in applied arts, design engineering, and a Ph.D. in biblical studies; and has done architectural plans and drawings for 30 years.

She is also the mother of three sons, plus one daughter; and has written and published three books of general collected poetry, A Passion for Poetry (2013), Passion Laughs Out Loud! (2015), and The Ruby Cat (2018). The books contain a combined total of over 5000 poems, ranking her as one of Michigan's most prolific published poets.

Ms. Garrison is also the recipient of the 1994 Best of Quill National Award for her poem, *Flowers*, first in a field of 3,000.

Ms. Garrison did the writing, compiling, and cover.

Both women have strong family ties and love the outdoors; both studied at and graduated from CMU; both are born again believers, saved at the age of five; and both have learned life-changing lessons from Sawyer's love-more / judge-less life style and his experience seeing God for who He is, his true faith and transparency with God.

Myra   Marilyn

VERSE INDEX

NOTES